Brodie Country

James Brodie

ISBN: 1503015726
ISBN-13: 9781503015722

INTRODUCTION

Doctor Johnson famously remarked that it requires no great abilities to be a historian. The facts being ready to hand, it requires little imagination and only a modicum of penetration and accuracy to relate them. I am grateful for the great man's opinion, since it perfectly reflects the state of blissful ignorance in which I embarked on this project.

The task proved to be larger than I had anticipated. It required a most detailed study of Scottish History in order to interpret the source material. It brought me into a happy familiarity with the resources of the British Library, the Public Records Office and various interesting archives. It also introduced me to numerous brave and accomplished men and women who happened to have borne the same surname. I am extremely glad to have met them.

I hope the reader will find the same pleasure in meeting them in these pages.

Jim Brodie,

Forres, May 1999.

CONTENTS

Brodie Castle

ACKNOWLEDGMENTS

It would be impossible to carry out a project of this type without a great deal of help from a large number of people. I must especially thank the staff of the British Library for their consistently helpful and professional service. I must also thank the staff of the Public Record Office, who are exemplary in all respects, and the Morayshire Library Service, who were most co-operative in supplying many quite rare items from their collection to me via the inter-library loan system.

My thanks are also due to Doctor Blackden, the Archivist at Brodie Castle, who kindly read and discussed the first draft with me. Finally, my warm appreciation to my family, whose unstinting help and support made the whole venture possible.

1: A VISIT TO KING BRUDE

There is a tradition that the name "Brodie" is derived from the followers of Brude, King of the Northern Picts, a Warlord who ruled much of Northern Scotland during the Sixth Century AD. Brude was converted to Christianity by Saint Columba. A history of the Saint's mission was subsequently written by the monk Adomnan, and survives today. These events took place in the summer of the year 565 AD. Brude died in battle in 584 AD, having lived and ruled from his fortress east of Inverness, in what is now "Brodie Country"

Scotland has been inhabited for more than six thousand years, and in its wild and open landscape the relics of its early inhabitants may still be seen, defying the passage of time and weather. In the earliest period of habitation, the Caledonian forest covered the land, interspersed with impenetrable swamp. The lives of the inhabitants need not have been brutish, however, for the climate was milder then than now. The clean seas and rivers abounded with fish, the coasts were home to millions of wild birds. Red Deer grazed the forests, and there was plentiful rich pasture for domesticated sheep and cattle.

Those unknown people left their monuments in the form of elaborate chambered tombs, still complete after thirty centuries, massively constructed to endure. This suggests some form of central authority, to organise these massive works, and an organised religion, as these structures were built in preparation for the afterlife. They built stone circles, perhaps as astronomical calendars, perhaps doubling as a meeting place or court. The enigmatic stones still stand, marking the border between prehistory and antiquity. They had military architecture, and some 400 of their defensive forts, known as Brochs, still remain. The common design of these forts over a wide geographical area argues for a united people facing a common threat, and the greatest concentration of them, in the North and East, suggests that the threat came from Scandinavia, a thousand years before the Vikings.

When the Roman Legions swept north through Britain, they named the ungovernable Caledonian tribesmen "Picti," meaning "the painted ones" or the "People of the designs," and their nickname has stuck. The "designs" seem to have been tattoos symbolic of the tribe and status of the wearer. They may have included the symbols we still see carved on Pictish memorial slabs. The Roman army fought its way through Scotland on several campaigns, and fought the tribe they called the "Borestii" on the Laigh of Moray, in "Brodie Country". The Picts fought with iron swords and spears, and their leaders rode into battle in war chariots drawn by two sturdy hill ponies. They carried small circular shields, the forerunner of the highlanders "Targe," but they wore no body armour, relying instead on the speed and fury of their attack. Roman writers speak of the unsettling effect of their braying war horns, and the blood curdling battle cry of the Picts as they charged. Eventually the Romans gave up their attempt at conquest, and built two walls across Britain from the Irish Sea to the North Sea. The walls were defended, overrun and recaptured at various times during four centuries when they marked the northernmost border of the Roman Empire.

Little is known of Pictish history, for the inscriptions on their carved memorials have defied interpretation, and their language, P-Celtic, exists only in place names and a smattering of words in the Gaelic that replaced it. The Irish annals record the names of seventy Pictish kings, their deeds briefly glimpsed in myth and legend. These were the centuries when the Angles, Britons, Picts, and Irish met in the "Dreadful Clashings of Wars" described by Adomnan. His history of Saint Columba gives us an insight into the land of the Picts in the middle part of the sixth Century AD

What is now Scotland was divided. North and south of the Grampian Mountains were the northern and southern Picts. In the south west were the Britons of Strathclyde and the Picts of Galloway. In the south east, a warrior chief of the Angles fortified the rock still known as Edwin's Burgh, and in the west, Argyll - the land of the Gael - was home to the Scotti, the Christian Irish, who were to give Scotland its name, its religion, and its royal house.

Conjecture can carry us back, to the villages of wattle huts where the sacred rowan bloomed in spring, and the old hag of winter, the *Cailleach*, brought war with her coming. When barns were packed with the harvest bounty, and the herds of cattle fattened against the coming frost, men would sharpen their spears and prepare for war.

The border between the Scots of Dalriada and the two kingdoms of the Picts is vague now, but 1400 years ago it was absolute, a boundary of language, culture, and religion. The Pictish kingdom of Alba was Druidic. Its people worshipped the sun, kept the feasts of Beltane (May Day) and Halloween, and revered the mistletoe. The priesthood stood higher in the social scale than the warrior ranks from which kings were drawn. A novitiate to this priestly caste might spend seven years learning the songs of tribal history, and so become a *bard*, qualified to create as well as recite the folk memory of his people, and hand on their traditions to later generations. Another seven years of study and the bard might become a *brehon*, a master of the law. In their system, no vagueness was allowed to intrude. Every man was party to myriad contracts, with his king, his wife, his tribe, his animals, and his gods. Were he to renege on any of his contractual duties, or even intend to renege, he could be punished, by death, fine, or banishment. A man who failed to prevent a crime was guilty of the crime. A man driven out was no man.

The third and highest priestly rank, the *Druid*, could be attained by another seven years of training. Here, the darkness is complete, for the mysteries of Druidism could not be written down, and the propaganda of Christian and Roman alike overlay our understanding of their creed. Certainly they were seers, and the tradition of second sight remained well into the twentieth century among the island peoples of the west. They were diviners, foretelling the future from natural signs, and again, the vestigial tradition has lingered into modern times. They were said to be able to direct wind and weather by charms and spells, to heal or injure at a distance, to make or lift curses. This part of their rites became debased into 'witchcraft', but there may once have been much beauty and wisdom in the teachings of the "Old Religion." There was little barbarism in the conversion to Christianity, only one of Christ's missionaries was martyred in the field. More bloodshed accompanied Scotland's interpretation of Christianity than ever stained its adoption of it.

Bridei, son of Maelcon, must have been aware of the existence and general character of the new religion, for he had variously treated with his Christian neighbours and slaughtered them. His father is believed to have been Maelgwn, a powerful Welsh king, it being the custom of Pictish women to choose the fathers of their children from men other than their husbands. This caused a great deal of prurient comment from Roman and Christian observers, but it was perfectly respectable in Pictish culture.

The Irish Annals record the *"Flight of the Scots before Brude, son of Maelcon"* in 560 AD. and the death of their King Gabran in the same year. This seems to signify a decisive victory of the Picts over the Dalriadan Scots, especially as no further fighting is recorded between them for fifteen years.

Bridei was then at the height of his power, with a kingdom that stretched from the Orkney Islands to the Tay, a fleet of warships, and a victorious army. There is evidence that he imposed his will by taking hostages against his subjects' good behaviour, and that he used some Roman techniques in the organisation of his forces. His survival and success testify to his ability. He held his court near Inverness, in what was to become Brodie country. His visitor, in 565 AD. was Saint Columba

Columba was born on December 5th, 521 AD. at Gartan, a wild and mountainous district of present day Donegal. He was an aristocrat, the great, great grandson of Niall of the Nine Hostings, High King of all Ireland at Royal Tara from 379 to 405 AD. One of Niall's slaves, a certain Patricius, had escaped to Gaul, and returned as a missionary, spreading the word of Christ throughout the Island kingdom. This man, Saint Patrick, created the school of piety and learning that was to produce Columba.

Columba left Ireland under a cloud. Legend tells that a ludicrous argument over the copying of a book of Psalms had let to bloodshed, and to Columba's excommunication, and that his mission was in atonement for his involvement. It seems more probable that he left for Scottish Dalriada to help his kinfolk there, who had just received the crushing blow from King Brude. Adomnan tells us:

"In the forty second year of his age, desiring to seek a foreign country for the sake of Christ, he sailed from Ireland to Britain. "

Columba's feelings at leaving his native land are recorded in an ancient Irish poem:

How rapid the speed of my coracle, and its stem turned upon Derry;

I grieve at my errand o 'er the noble sea, travelling to Alba of the ravens,

My foot in my sweet little coracle, my sad heart still bleeding:

Weak is the man that cannot lead, totally blind are all the ignorant.

There is a grey eye, that looks back upon Erin;

It shall not see during life the men of Erin, nor their wives.

My vision o 'er the brine I stretch, from the ample oaken planks;

Large is the tear of my soft grey eye, when I look back upon Erin.

The journey from Antrim to the Mull of Kintyre is barely twelve miles, but that must have been a considerable voyage in a Curragh of wicker and hide, laden with twelve followers and all their provisions. Columba visited his family in Argyll, then sailed north, landing, eventually, on a small but sheltered rocky island in the Inner Hebrides, on the border between Christian Dalriada and the heathen Picts. On that island, Iona, Columba and his followers constructed their oaken church and their wicker huts. Sixty kings are now buried on that most revered of islands, and it has been a place of pilgrimage for more than a thousand years.

When the monastery school of Iona had been established to his satisfaction, Columba resolved to begin his mission to the pagan court of King Brude. He chose two companions, Kenneth and Comgall, who were themselves Pictish and spoke Brude's language. Together they were to face the *"Perils of water, perils of robbers, perils by the heathen, perils of the wilderness,"* known to the Apostles of old. They travelled through the Glen Mhor Nan Albin, the "Great Glen of Alban", the diagonal rift that runs north east through Scotland from Lismore to the River Ness. Travellers were few along the frontier route, beneath the dark brooding mountains and through the tangled forests. It is hard for our modern minds to conceive nature as the early Christians and Pagans saw it. By our standards, the fertile Glen would have been teeming with wildlife. The Lochs were sparkling clean and alive with large healthy fish. The sky home to a myriad of fowl, from the skylark to the great Golden Eagle, their cries echoing from the hills all day long, and the woods well populated with large animals and small, from the badger to the bear, from the weasel to the wild boar. Threading the paths along the Lochs, not only the visible wildlife would have affected the party, but the invisible too. In Pagan belief, every spring and stream, tree and rock, had its own resident spirit. The pagans believed in these spirits and worshipped them as local deities. The Christians believed in them and loathed them as demons. To both belief systems, Columba's party was a challenge, an encroachment, and they could expect attack from the material and invisible worlds as they approached their goal. One such clash with a local demon is now considered the earliest recorded encounter with the still - disputed lake creature called "The Loch Ness Monster." In the words of the Monk Adomnan:

When the blessed man was obliged to cross the River Ness,..... he met some of the inhabitants burying an unlucky fellow...who had been seized and savagely bitten by an aquatic monster while swimming...and whose body had been rescued too late by his companions. The Saint, upon hearing these things, ordered one of his companions to swim across and bring back a small boat that was beached on the other bank. And hearing and obeying the command of the holy and illustrious man, Lugne Mocumin takes off his clothes, all but his tunic, and casts himself into the water. But the monster, which was lying on the river bed...suddenly comes up and moves toward the man as he swam in mid stream, and with a great roar rushes on him with open mouth while all who were there, Barbarians as well as Brethren, were struck with terror. Then the Saint made the sign of the cross in the air and commanded the monster, saying " Go no further nor touch the man, go back at once!" ...on hearing this word of the Saint... the monster was terrified... and fled as quickly as if dragged off by ropes ... though it had been as close to Lugne as the length of one punt pole. Lugne returned to them safely in the boat ...and even the heathens present ... magnified the God of the Christians.

The River Ness, where this encounter is said to have occurred, is the outlet of Loch Ness to the Moray Firth on which Inverness is built. Celtic mythology speaks of numerous Lake and River monsters, known in Scotland as *water horses*, and two of them, in Loch Ness and Loch Morar, are widely believed to exist. Certainly there is a substantial body of circumstantial evidence, obscure photographs, and eye witness reports. These are displayed in a visitor centre by the Loch, and seem to indicate something, perhaps an enormous eel, perhaps something more, has bred successfully and evaded capture throughout the fourteen centuries since it was first reported to the Saint. There are surviving Pictish carvings that show the familiar profile of the "Sea Serpent", and there are many people living around the Loch who honestly believe that they have seen the creature as depicted. At dusk, when the wind ruffles the reflections of the mountains in the surface of the thousand foot deep Loch, it is easy to believe, and the peat-darkened waters do not suggest a cosy or friendly presence, but something primeval and cold.

The location of Brudes fortress is a subject of speculation. The fact that the Saint had to cross the River Ness seems to indicate that it was East of the River, and there is a hill, now in the town of Inverness itself, called "The Crown" where tradition says the first Castle stood. There are other candidates for the site, however, including Brodie Castle itself The Pictish Cross Slab found nearby must have been erected to commemorate something significant; but a King needs a capital, and the largest town east of the Ness in those days was Forres. This appeared on Ptolomy's map in the second century AD as "Varies" (Pictish Far-ius, near the water), and it was already a considerable town in Brude's time. There is an account of some merchants being executed, and their stock confiscated, at Forres in 535 AD, which suggests overseas trade and a regulatory authority, both hallmarks of a regional capital. So it may well have been at Forres, four miles from Brodie, that Columba met the King.

Columba was not made welcome on his arrival. As the travel - weary missionaries reached the stockade King Brude, no doubt on the advice of his foster father, the Chief Druid Broichan, caused the gates of the fortress to be closed against them. Columba walked up to the gates, traced the sign of the cross upon them, and then knocked. At once the bolts flew back of their own accord and the gates burst open. The party entered, and Brude and his warriors, much disturbed by this demonstration of Columbas power, hurried forward to greet them.

Brude would not listen to the missionaries until he had satisfied himself as to their wisdom. He asked each of the three companions to solve a riddle. To Comgall, he said; *"What is more numerous than the blades of grass?"* Comgall replied, *"The dew drops upon them, your majesty."* Brude nodded, then turned to Kenneth: *"What is whiter than new-fallen snow?"* Kenneth replied, *"the purity of a child, your majesty."* Brude nodded again. Finally he turned to Columba and asked, *"What is hotter than the hottest fire?"* The conventional reply was about loss of honour, but Columba ignored it and replied sharply; *"The shame of a man who fails in his duty of hospitality to strangers."* Brude stared at him, not sure whether to take offence. He did not. He suddenly burst into laughter and ordered his servants to set a meal for the visitors... *"and from that day forth "* says Adomnan *"this ruler honoured the holy and venerable man with very great honour all the remaining days of his life. "*

During his stay with Brude, Columba saw evidence of his power. One Pict is described as the "Captain of a Cohort," suggesting Roman influence in the organisation of the Pictish Army. Messengers arrive on horseback from the farthest territories of the Kingdom. There is a King's Council and a Royal treasury. There is a hierarchical Druidic priesthood, governed by Brude's foster father, the Chief Druid Broichan. The son's of lesser chiefs live at the court as respected guests, but they are not permitted to leave. The people of the Kingdom live in normal family units, but Irish slaves supplied by Brude's victorious army do the domestic work.

Columba's mission to King Brude was spectacularly successful. The old ruler listened carefully to the Saint and offered his support, even confirming the rights of the Christian community on Iona and undertaking to guarantee their tenure there. However, the old chief did not invite Columba to build his church locally. Perhaps the activities of another religious sect, on a remote island far to the west, did not concern him much. Bridei's Druidic religion was inherently tolerant, recognising that all the gods, even new ones, have power and need to be accommodated. Columba was less successful with Broichan the Druid, who did all he could to hinder the newcomers.

Broichan may have been more perceptive than his obliging foster son. The teachings of the Christians were hostile to the established order. Their God would tolerate no competition, and they advocated humility and pacifism, unhelpful characteristics in a warrior King. This was not the addition of another god to the pantheon of Norse, Roman and home-grown deities that had their adherents on the Laigh. This was a take-over bid, which if successful would destroy the old religion. One area of conflict between them was Columba's request to Broichan to free a slave, a young Irish Christian girl, who may have been captured during Brude's raids into Dalriada. The Mage stubbornly refused to let the slave free, and Columba mildly warned Broichan that if he did not give the girl up he would quickly die. Soon afterwards, sitting in a field with his followers, Columba remarked that a drinking glass had just burst in Broichan's hands and that he was close to death.

Within minutes, the Kings messengers arrived to tell Columba that Broichan was dying, and to beg his help. Columba ensured that the slave girl would be freed, and then sent a pebble, blessed by him, to be put in a cup of water for the Druid to drink. He warned that the pebble would cure Broichan if he intended to keep his promise, but kill him instantly if he did not. The girl was freed, and the Druid returned to health.

This did not stir any feelings of gratitude in the old Mage. On hearing that the Missionaries intended to return to Iona by boat down Loch Ness, Broichan promised to conjure a storm. Adomnan writes:

"On the same day as he had purposed in his heart the saint came to the long lake of the River Ness, a great crowd following. But the druids began to rejoice when they saw a great darkness coming over, and a contrary wind with a tempest. Nor should it be wondered that these

things can be done by the art of demons, God permitting it, so that even winds and waters are roused to fury. Our Columba therefore...calls upon Christ the Lord, and entering the boat while the sailors hesitated, orders the sails to be rigged against the wind, which being done...the boat is borne along against the wind with amazing velocity... and after no great interval, the winds veer round and become gentle favouring breezes, which bear them to their desired haven. "

So ended Columba's first mission to King Brude, and our only window into the world of the Northern Picts. The ancient Abbey of Saint Benedict at Fort Augustus now marks the "desired haven" at which Columba completed his journey. The legacy of King Brude may be in the world-wide genetic heritage of his followers, who remain, for the most part. Christian.

2. THE MUCKLE BURN

The view across the Moray plain from the road outside Nairn is one of the most beautiful in Scotland. A rich and fertile strip of land fringes the sea, dotted with farms and prosperous small villages. The climate is so mild that the area has long been known as "The garden and granary of Scotland" The surrounding mountains give shelter from the prevailing westerly winds, and intercept much of the winter rain, helping to make Moray Scotland's sunniest coast. There are said to be thirty more days of summer here than in the rest of Scotland.

Beyond the Firth the distant hills of Cromarty and Dornoch rise blue above the horizon. To the west and south the encircling highlands, with high moors between, purple and brown with their shawl of heather. Close by, the River Nairn winds it's way through forests of Beech and Oak, and down through the ancient fisher town to the old harbour. Along the way it passes Cawdor Castle, the scene of Shakespeare's tragedy of Macbeth. King Duncan remarked, in the play "This Castle hath a pleasant seat" and indeed, it still has. Looking east, the green sweep of Culbin forest contrasts with the deep blue of the summer firth, to the west, the roofs of Inverness, "The capital of the highlands"; but this is not a highland scene. The Laigh, or plain, of Moray is an arm of the fertile lowlands, running east to west along the south shore of the firth, hemmed in by the highlands and the sea.

The history of Scotland has been determined by geography. Eighty per cent of the land is rugged corrugations of ancient rock, riven and split into mountain and glen. The mountains catch the rain from the winds that blow in from the Atlantic three hundred days of the year, and hold the water in the thousands of lochs and lochans, tarns and bogs, rivers and rivulets, waterfalls and burns. It is a landscape of barriers, of water and rock. Areas that are a few miles apart as the eagle flies are only accessible by days of walking, or hard climbing to a saddle among the peaks that becomes known as a pass. These natural barriers restricted communication between the highland communities, and became, in time, the territorial basis for the Clan system.

There are three main access routes through the highlands: Glen Mhor, the Great Glen that splits the land diagonally from Loch Linnhe to the Ness, and the western routes to the sea by Glen Moriston in the south, Glen Carron and Strath Conon further north. All three routes lead to Inverness, which forms a gateway between the rugged highlands and the fertile farmlands of Moray. The mountains of southern Moray were known as *Braemoray*, to distinguish them from the lowlands of the Laigh. The mountains feed three major river systems that lead down to the plain: the Nairn, the Findhom, and the Spey. These have been used, time out of mind, as routes for highland raiders to attack the rich farmlands of the Laigh, as recalled in this "translation from the Gaelic";

Round the rock, down by the Knock,

Monnaughty, Tannachty, Moy and Glentrive

Brodie and Balloch and Ballindalloch,

Shall pay kane to the king belyve.

'Kane' is the old word for rent in 'kind' (goods), otherwise known as 'blackmail'. Most of the places named are on the plain, all of them were estates that held out against the Jacobite rebellions of the eighteenth century... but that comes later. In the beginning there were warrior farmers on the Laigh, that produced metal goods and raised their families in stockaded villages, close to the rivers. Souvenirs of the times may still be found when the sea washes away the dunes north of Culbin, exposing the rich black soil beneath the sand. Local collections indicate the products of those communities. The earliest relics are the arrowheads and knife blades made of flint. Later came crucibles and moulds for metalworking, and the products of the craftsmen. Swords and axes, of course, but arm bracelets and brooches, too, rings and bangles and coloured glass beads, dress fasteners and cutlery. The early settlers on the Laigh had all nature's bounty around them, and their lives, in the unspoiled landscape, must have had a quality that we can scarcely

imagine.

One such settlement was raised on the level, well-wooded ground beside the Muckle Burn, a tributary of the Findhom. There the people found good grazing for their animals, and good land for their crops. They had fine timber, and a wealth of salmon and trout in the clean waters of the burn. There was easy access to the sea where the burn met the Findhom, and a natural defence in the river crossings. It may be that no other tribe ever occupied that piece of the earth, still held today by the oldest untitled landed family in Britain, the main stem of the clan, or family, of Brodie.

The name may, it is said, be derived from the clay soil of the area, giving *Brothaig*, a muddy place, or ditch. Certainly the parish and village are called Dyke, which also means ditch. Well, mud sticks, and we can scarcely object to being named for the clay that bred us. Other, perhaps wiser, academics have found the likely origin of the name to be that of Brude, warrior King of the Northem Picts, who ruled much of Scotland, and even the Orkney Islands, from a fortress in these parts during the sixth century. Brude had a properly organised army and a fleet of war galleys, and he kept peace throughout his kingdom by taking hostages from the families of local leaders. He was the hammer of the Gaelic invaders, and yet he was merciful. He gave the island of Iona to Saint Columba to help him with his Christian mission. It would be delightful to prove the Brudes as the ancestors of the Brodies, but we can not. From Bridei, son of Maelcon, who died in 584 AD to Malcolm Brodie, died 1285, there is a gap in the written record, but for one enigmatic message: The Pictish cross stone in the grounds of Brodie Castle, said to date from the seventh century AD. On one face, the Christian symbol carved in ornate Celtic knotwork. On the other, the designs of the Picts, that gave them their name. In the pattem of these carvings we may be looking at the characteristic tattoos of our farthest known ancestors. The cryptic message, in Ogham script, may never be translated.

The Muckle Burn is a clean and swift flowing stream, a smaller model of the Findhom itself. It rises at 400 metres on the slopes of Caim a Chrasgie, behind the Cawdor woods. From there it leaps and sparkles through heather covered moorland, the leafy canopy of the Darnaway forest, and the sunlit farmlands of the Laigh before joining the Findhom in the deep tidal inlet of Findhom Bay. All along it's route it passes through landscapes rich with Brodie family history. The Burn has many names, including the Lethen Burn, the Dalvey Burn, the Earlsmill Burn, the Dyke Burn, and the Brodie Burn. All the names are associated with the Brodies, and all have a tale to tell. The Muckle Burn has been the scenic background to a thousand years of our family history.

At Earlsmill the burn emerges from the Darnaway forest and passes close to Macbeth's Hillock in the grounds of Brodie Castle. This is the wooded knoll where the three witches are said to have met the Thane of Cawdor and prophesied his elevation and destruction. It has been a tourist attraction since Shakespeare's play was first performed, and even Johnson and Boswell gave an impromptu performance beneath its trees when they came here in 1773.

It is easy to imagine the meeting. A canopy of fir casts its gloomy shade over the dry, scrubby ground. The black trunks and the dismal scrub merge to form lurking places for the night creatures. Cast your mind back a thousand years and gaze out across the moor, to where Macbeth and Banquo are returning from battle to report to King Duncan at his camp at Forres. Their battered armour is splashed with blood, after winning victory from horror on "So fair and foul a day" as they had ever seen. They see the three hags on the knoll:

How far is't called to Forres?

What are these, so withered and so wild in their attire,

That look not like the inhabitants of the earth, and yet are on it?

Live you? Or are you aught that man may question?

You seem to understand me

By each at once her chappy finger laying

Upon her skinny lips...

...and the witches tell their fortune. The real Macbeth must have passed this spot many times. Macbeth was Mormaer, or Earl, of Moray for eleven years before he became King. He became Mormaer by burning his predecessor, Gillacomgan, to death, along with fifty of his men, and he gained the throne by defeating Duncan in battle, not murdering him in his bed. He ruled Scotland successfully for seventeen years, and was secure enough in his kingdom to go on a pilgrimage to Rome, where he scattered money like corn among the poor. He was eventually defeated in battle at Lumphanon in 1057 by Adam Gourdon of Quercy; a French knight then in service with King Duncan's eldest son, Malcolm. Gourdon was rewarded with land, and became the progenitor of the powerful Gordon Clan. They were to be uncomfortable neighbours for the Brodies of Brodie for several centuries.

Macbeth was the last of the Celtic Kings of Scotland. Malcolm III, and his saintly wife Margaret, introduced many Norman institutions into the country, including feudalism. This was a system of Social control by which all the land of the country was owned by the King, and held by the nobles in return for armed service in time of war. The nobles could sub-let land in return for services, and so down the social scale to the peasant, who held his small farm in exchange for rents paid out of his produce. It was the fusion of this system with the older Celtic traditions of kinship that gave the Scottish Clan system its particular character. The feudal lord was both the King's direct representative, with Royal powers over his subjects, and also the chief in the Celtic tradition. The head of the clan combined the power "of pit and gallows" over his followers with family ties and responsibilities to every one of them. The new system did not take root North and West of The Great Glen, where the 'Lords of the Isles' existed as a virtually independent country.

The Celtic chiefs of Moray who rebelled against the new system lost their lands, and the incoming Normans took control not only of the acreage, but also the paternalistic leadership of their tenants. Malcolm IV, the great grandson of Duncan, confirmed the Brodie's title to their lands in 1160, but they were not Norman incomers...monastic records a century earlier refer to them as "long established". They must have wondered at the grim strangers that were taking control of the surrounding lands. The first Normans treated their tenants as possessions to be used, rather than kinsmen to be led and cared for. New castles were raised on the Laigh, wooden stockades on high earth "Mottes", built to defend the owners from their own tenants as well as from their fellow Norman neighbours. There is no motte at Brodie. The kinsmen of the Thane were wall enough to his foes, and no threat to his person.

Many of the great families of Scotland arrived at this time. The Frasiers, destined to become Clan Fraser, took up residence in Glen Moriston, and the Grants, followers of a Norman called Bisset, moved in to Strath Spey. A great family called de Soulis brought the family of Hay in their train. The King needed powerful allies to keep down the rebellions in Moray, so he elevated the Norman family of Comyn to become his representative rulers in the North east, with virtually all of Buchan, Badenoch and Moray under their sway. King Malcolm had valuable estates in England, but to keep them he had to acknowledge the English King Henry II as his feudal superior. This was to prove disastrous for the cause of Scottish Independence. In 1157 Malcolm (who is remembered as "The Maiden") even allowed Henry to Knight him, an abject gesture in a supposedly independent Monarch. The Scots Lords rebelled at this humiliation, and had to be suppressed by force. The date of the Brodie's Charter, 1160, seems to indicate that the family stayed loyal during the rebellion, or at least stayed out of it. Or perhaps they did rebel, but were received into the Kings peace on submission. The records from those times were all destroyed when Brodie was burned in 1645..

Alexander III confirmed Malcolm, Thane of Brodie, in his tenure of the lands of Brodie and Dyke, before 1285. The Thane of Dyke had been a Macbeth in 1262, so the Brodie added Macbeth's lands to his own and probably helped to remove him from the property. Scotland at this time was a mixed society whose land-owning classes might be of Pictish, Norman, Irish, English or Flemish origin. Gaelic and Pictish customs merged with the Norman ways, and, gradually, a distinctively "Scottish" culture emerged. The Norman title of Earl replaced the Celtic Mormaer, and the Gaelic title of Taesoch, or Chief, was replaced with "Thane".

The great historian of Moray, Lachlan Shaw, suggests that the Brodies, the Innes' and the Murrays (De Moray) were all ancient families of local extraction who continued to thrive after the Norman incursions. He supports this by pointing out that all three families have similar coats of arms containing three stars. We do know that there have been Brodies at Brodie for at least a thousand years, and perhaps much longer.

Alexander III died on a stormy night in March 1286. He had been riding home, after some hard drinking, to his young wife. He lost the path in the dark, resulting in a fall from his horse and a broken neck. A famous "seer" Thomas the Rhymer, had seen skeletons dancing at Alexander's wedding feast, but this was not a purely domestic tragedy. The heir apparent was a sickly girl child, who died before her coronation, leaving the throne of Scotland empty. There were thirteen candidates for the crown, all men of blood, but the strongest claims were those of the Bruce, Comyn and Balliol factions.

The contenders asked King Edward I of England to arbitrate. Edward agreed to judge the claimants' cases and rule on who should be King. He also arranged the armed occupation of Scotland by English garrisons while he thought the matter over. He eventually selected the weaker candidate, Balliol, to be his puppet King. Edward went a shade too far in his studied humiliations of Balliol, and eventually forced him into rebellion. Edward then led his army into Scotland and massacred the citizens of Berwick, leaving their unburied corpses to rot in the street as a warning to the Scots. He defeated Balliol's' army with contemptuous ease, arrested the "King", and ordered all the landed gentry of Scotland to attend the sacked city of Berwick (still strewn with corpses) to swear allegiance to him. The monumental document produced by this procedure, hung with innumerable seals and signatures but ultimately worthless, is known as the "Ragman's Roll", and is the origin of the word "rigmarole". The Thane of Brodie added his seal to the roll, and the Clan badge of Brodie may still be seen there, pledging the submission of "The Brodies and their Ilk" to the Norman tyrant. It is said that Edward only called a halt to the sack of Berwick when he saw a pregnant woman giving birth as she was hacked to death in the street. We can imagine the rage that burned in the breast of Malcolm, Thane of Brodie, as he rode among the evidence of such atrocities.

Edward is still remembered as "The Hammer of the Scots." His hammering served to forge them into a nation. It had been common for Scottish magnates to hold estates in England, to be equivocal in their loyalties, to see their interests as being quite distinct from those of their fellow countrymen. The occupation itself defined all as Scots, and the Scots as a people without liberty. The stage was set for the great drama that brought Scotland its Independence. It needed only the hero, and he proved heroic beyond the expected bounds of humanity. The greatest champion of Scottish liberty, William Wallace.

Wallace was a giant by the standards of the time. He was more than two metres tall, a superb swordsman, and, it seems, a likeable man who inspired friendship in those he met. He was of relatively humble birth, which did not endear him to the Magnates. Both Robert the Bruce and the Comyns fought for Edward against Wallace. Above all, William seems to have appealed to the common folk, and he taught them their greatest lesson; how to defeat the heavy cavalry by which the English dominated the battlefield.

The great war-horses of the Normans, called "Destriers" had no equivalent in the North. They were extremely expensive, and required better grazing than Scottish fields could readily afford. In battle, the armoured horse and rider were devastating. Edward could put literally thousands of them into the field of battle, and Wallace's irregulars could not be expected to stand before them...until Wallace developed the *Schiltron*. This was a troop formation, the forerunner of the Infantry Square. A tight packed mass of spearmen with spears facing outward, like a giant steel tipped hedgehog. When time permitted, the ground in front of the Schiltron would be dug with small covered pits to trip the Destriers, and the butts of the spears would be embedded into the earth, so that they would hold against an impact until the shaft snapped. The most determined cavalry charge against a prepared Schiltron would end in a nightmare of screaming, disembowelled horses and fallen riders. Once the heavily encumbered knights were thrown down, they were easily despatched with knife, axe, or sword.

By May 1297, a national uprising had begun. Wallace himself began it with a bloody act of vengeance. He burst into the home of the English Sheriff of Lanark, William Heselrig, and slew him in his bed. Heselrig was a particularly nasty piece of work, even by mediaeval standards, notoriously cruel and oppressive to the native Scots. He had murdered Wallace's eighteen-year-old bride, Marion Braidfute. Wallace split the Sheriff's skull with one blow of his broadsword, and killed his only son on the way out. The killings were the signal for a general uprising. More than two hundred English men died in Lanark that night, and the English women, children and clergy were driven from the town. Wallace tried to temper extreme violence with chivalry, and his refusal to make war on non-combatant's contrasts strangely with Edward's methods. Within a few weeks of the death of Heselrig, Wallace's guerrilla band had become an army.

News of Wallace's early success spread rapidly through the country, bringing a hope of liberty to the enslaved Scots. Yet it was not the Bruce, or the Comyn, that was the first among the Magnates to join the rebellion. It was Andrew de Moray, of the three stars of Moray, and he brought the men of Moray with him. Andrew had been captured at the battle of Dunbar, and had been imprisoned in Chester Castle. He was eventually released, and made his way home to the Laigh of Moray. His journey took him through the war-ravaged country of Cumbria and Galloway, where he must have seen and spoken with many of his contemporaries, including Wallace. He reached home in the spring of 1297. He found the Moray plain dominated by the English garrisons in the castles of Inverness, Nairn, Forres, Elgin, Urquhart and Lochindorb. Andrew raised his standard on the Black Isle, and sent out the fiery cross to summon the common army of the Scots. From Nairn and Forres, Elgin and Banff, Brodie and Auldearn, the men of Moray flocked to his standard. Andrew's army consisted almost entirely of the common folk of Moray, organised and led by the minor gentry. We can not doubt that the Brodie's were among them, especially as Brodie was subsequently burned in reprisal. By mid summer almost all of the Laigh had been taken back by the Scots, and most of the English garrisons had surrendered. Edward sent John Comyn of Badenoch to quell the rebellion, and he lay waste and burned the villages of Damaway and

Drakies, Brodie and Dyke, Kyntessack, Altyre and Balnaferry. The Comyns were accustomed, like Edward, to rule by terror, but they were already too late. The men of Moray had met and joined with Wallace's army on the Spey. They were already marching south, to meet Edward's Army on the Carse of Stirling.

The battle was fought at the river crossing of Stirling Bridge. The bridge was narrow and would allow only two horsemen abreast to cross it. As the English Army, at the behest of it's hated treasurer, Cressingham, tried to cross without first securing a bridgehead, Wallace's spearmen attacked in a furious downhill charge. They trapped the English against the bank and maintained a fearsome hacking assault, driving them back into the river. The English army was broken and its baggage train sacked. Cressingham was flayed, some say alive, and his hide used to make a sheath for Wallace's sword. Fragments of his skin were sent all over the country as token of the victory. It was the first triumph of a united Scotland against their southern neighbours. Wallace was later betrayed and captured, and the leadership passed to Robert the Bruce. The Brodies supported The Bruce during his struggle for the Scottish Crown, and he issued a charter confirming Michael as Thane of Brodie and Dyke in 1311. Michael was the son of Malcolm that received the charter from Alexander III. The Bruce campaigned along the Moray Firth during the winter of 1307 - 08, from his lands around Forres, on Brodie's doorstep. One of his chief officers during the campaign was Alan Moray of Culbin, Brodie's next door neighbour. The Bruce had been released from his wars with England by the sudden death of Edward I in the summer of 1307, and took advantage of the respite to destroy the Comyns, his rivals to the throne. He captured Inverness, and burned the castles of Nairn and Duffus. He destroyed the power of the Comyns, laid waste much of the north east, and went on to defeat all domestic opposition to his reign. His subsequent defeat of the English at Bannockburn gave Scotland real independence at last. Robert the Bruce was very thorough in destroying his opponents, and he showed no mercy even to the civil populations of his enemies' territory. The granting of the charter to Michael Brodie shows the Bruce's approval, and Michael was feudally bound to give military service. He must have served throughout the campaign.

The Bruce had cause to write to Michael Brodie in later years, to tell him to repair his mill pond, as his father had done in the previous reign, and keep it repaired. The complaint to the king had come from the Prior of Pluscarden Abbey, owners of the mill, who must have failed to move Brodie without the King's aid. The letter is now one of the treasures of Brodie Castle.

Following these campaigns the Bruce made his nephew, Thomas Randolph, the Earl of Moray. He became Brodie's feudal superior, and the virtual King of all Northern Scotland. Randolph built a castle at Damaway, two miles south of Brodie, and included a fine banqueting hall with a hammer beam roof that may still be seen today. Randolph had acquired all the lands previously ruled by the Comyns, and naturally continued his uncle's work of extirpating them. The scene of one of their battles is now a popular beauty spot on the Findhom River still called "Randolph's Leap."

The Findhom is beautiful throughout it's length, but nowhere more so than on the stretch where the tributary waters of the Dorback and Divie meet the main river. The banks are high and rocky, of granite and gneiss, heavily wooded and rich with wild flowers. The rocky gorge forces the river into a succession of deep pools and churning rapids. It still makes a formidable obstacle. It was here that Earl Randolph led a ferocious assault on a band of Comyn Clansmen led by Comyn of Raites and the heroic Alistair Ban (The Fair) of Dunphail.

Comyn of Raites had gathered his followers at Lethen, between the Findhom and the Muckle Bum. They marched down the valley of the Muckle Burn, where they fell into an ambush set by Earl Randolph at Whitemire, barely a mile from Darnaway. Raites was killed and the Comyns forced to retreat towards the Findhorn Gorge. Alistair Ban rallied his men on the bank, but found the opposite shore held by a large force of Randolph's men. They were heavily outnumbered, and Alistair knew his exhausted men could not hold out for long. He took up the Comyn standard and threw it across the gorge into the enemy ranks. He then cried *"Let the bravest keep it!"* and leapt across the gorge to land by the standard in the midst of the foe. His followers leapt after him above the roaring torrent, and hacked their way through to safety. Comyn of

Raites was buried where he had fallen in the ambush, and a cairn of stones raised to mark his grave. Randolph's epitaph to his fallen enemy was brief: *"There"* he said, *"I have buried the plague of Moray."*

The Comyns took shelter in Dunphail castle, under the leadership of Alistair Ban's father. Randolph regrouped his forces and laid siege to Dunphail, intending to starve them out. His plans were thwarted once more by the chief's son, Alistair Ban, who escaped from the castle with some of his men, dressed as peasants, and acquired enough meal to supply the defender's needs. They loaded the sacks of meal on sleds, and made their way to the camp of Randolph's army, where they claimed to be merchants, and asked for protection from the wicked Comyn freebooters. They were allowed to pass. A deep moat separated the castle bounds from the besieger's camp, and the peasants parked the loaded sleds against the slope opposite the sallyport of the castle. They unhitched the horses, and then, at a signal, pushed the sleds over the edge, leapt on to their horses, and rode from the camp. Comyn's men ran from the sallyport and grabbed the precious sacks.

Randolph was furious. He rode with his men in pursuit of Alistair and captured one of his followers. They soon forced him to divulge the secret of Alistair's hiding place, a cave in the river valley at Slaginnan. They piled brushwood at the entrance to the cave, and lit an enormous bonfire to suffocate Alistair and his followers. They cut the heads from the bodies and took them back to Dunphail. They used the beseiger's mangonel to throw the heads into the castle, finally sending the head of Alistair Ban over the parapet. It struck the earth close to where his father stood. The blonde hair was immediately recognisable and the old chief picked his son's head up from the dirt while bitter tears scalded his cheeks. Randolph shouted his triumph : *"Alistair has brought you meal, I send you meat to eat with it!"*. The Comyn Chief looked long at his beloved son's head before answering. *"It is a bitter morsel"* replied the old man *"but I will gnaw the last bone of it ere I surrender!"*

The Comyn stronghold of Dunphail still stands in the valley of the Dorback, a tributary of the Findhorn, about five miles south of Brodie. The castle is a picturesque ruin on a steep rocky eminence, the moat still clearly visible. A mound known locally as the *"Grave of the headless*

Comyns" was excavated during the eighteenth century, and found to contain several headless skeletons in stone coffins. The grave mound of Comyn of Raites, buried after the ambush, may still be seen at Whitemire. Randolph's terse epitaph was long remembered by a local tradition that if the grave were ever opened, a plague would escape and ravage Moray.

John Brodie (de Brothy) is recorded as attending on the Earl of Mar, Lieutenant of the North, in 1376. This was during the reign of the first Stewart King, Robert. Although the great-nephew of the Bruce, Robert was incompetent, and there was anarchy again. *"In those days "* it was recalled *"there was no law in Scotland...and justice was sent into banishment".* Alexander Stewart, the king's illegitimate son burned much of the country around Brodie in those years. He is still remembered as "The Wolf of Badenoch".

Stewart was then the Earl of Buchan, and in theory the Justiciar of the North. His base was an island castle in the middle of Lochindorb, twelve miles south of Brodie at the head of the Dorback. The castle had fomerly been a stronghold of the Comyns, and had been captured and used as a base by King Edward I of England during his invasion of 1303. The Stewarts had acquired the castle after the destruction of the Comyns by the Bruce. There the 'Wolf' gathered a band of *"Wild Wicked Helandmen"*, bound to his service by the unconditional servitude known as "Manrent". This was a form of feudal bondage by which masterless men attached themselves to a leader, and depended on him for their survival, protection and reward. In return they had to carry out his orders unconditionally. Stewart used them to plunder the surrounding countryside.

The Earl of Moray at the time was John Dunbar, who was married to the King's sister, and was thereby the Wolfs uncle. There was not much family affection between them. When the Earl put on a jousting competition in the grounds of Damaway Castle, he did not invite the Stewart. The Wolf turned up all the same, with his force of *Wild Wicked Helandmen* at his back. An ugly scene developed, and the Wolf was forced to return to his lair. There he heard that Bishop Burgh of Moray had excomunicated him. The Bishop may have wanted to bring the

Stewart to repentance, but he pushed him over the edge and into open rebellion.

The marauders swept down from the hills on to the Moray plain, burning, looting and murdering without pity. They put the torch to Elgin Cathedral, destroying not only the fabric of the building, but its treasure house of ancient charters and records. They burned large sections of Elgin and razed Forres. They plundered the monks of Pluscarden Abbey, before returning to the Wolfs Lair in the mountains. They deliberately destroyed Church property, and the houses of numerous church officials, to punish Bishop Burgh.

Eventually, the Wolf was tamed, not by the characteristic violence of the times, but by his own fear of hell. The Little Cross in Elgin High Street is said to mark the very spot where the Wolf went down on his knees and begged forgiveness of The Lord. He was reconciled publicly with Bishop Burgh, at Ruthven Castle in 1380, and John of Brodie was there to watch them embrace. It must have been a gratifying spectacle.

The Wolf's mountain lair is accessible today from the back road that runs from Forres to Dava Moor. The area is marshy, bleak and windswept, with few trees. Heather covered slopes reach away from the Loch to the rounded peaks of the surrounding hills, bare beneath the huge sky. The Island covers about an acre, and the ruined castle walls rise sheer from the waters edge, with the remnants of four round towers at the corners. There was said to be a secret causeway, that zig-zagged a few feet below the surface of the Loch and was known only to the wolf and his followers, but the clear waters reveal no trace of it today. The remains of the keep, built from granite and with a round tower at one end, still stands guard over the windswept loch and the featureless moor. It is a place of ghosts, even on a sunny day.

Stewart is remembered for his particular brand of savagery, but he was by no means the only rampaging wolf to sweep down from the highlands. A mile or two back towards Brodie, at Ardclach on the Findhorn, there is a neat little church nestling in a pretty glen, but it lacks a bell tower. The tower was built instead on the hillside above the village, where a twenty four-hour watch could be kept on the highlands, and the bells rung to warn the country when the *Wild Wicked Helandmen* were approaching. During one attack the highlanders cut down the bells and threw them into the river, no doubt in frustration at finding the defenders prepared. The Bell Pool is now a good fishing spot in a valley of unparalleled beauty. The tower still provides a magnificent view of this beautiful, and now peaceful, part of Scotland.

For centuries the necessity for farming communities to remain in a high state of defensive preparation, and to suffer blackmail and murder at the hands of the Clan barons, held back social progress. However they are romanticised today, the disaffected clans were a force for chaos and oppression. Under the feudal system the Brodie held his land by charter from the King. In return he owed the King his allegiance, his armed support in war and the fulfilment of the Kings laws in his own lands. The accessibility of Morayshire meant that failing the King would lead to a swift reckoning with royal power. However inconvenient this may have been for the wilder early Thanes, it brought the rule of law and a degree of social stability to the area. In the more remote Highland areas and the western Isles, the chiefs were a law unto themselves. The Macdonald "Lords of the Isles" were able to operate virtually as an independent kingdom. They made regular forays into their neighbours' lands in quest of plunder and territorial power, and these were not mere cattle raids. In 1411, they swept down from the hills and attacked Inverness with an army of six thousand men.

No record exists of the Brodie's actions during the Macdonald's attack, although their feudal obligations and the need to protect their own lands left them no option but to fight. John of Brodie was received by the Earl of Mar after the battle, so we know that he played his part. Perhaps they fought to protect Inverness; perhaps their first knowledge of the attack was the column of smoke or the glow in the night sky as the town, the castle and the great Oak Bridge over the Ness burned. When the highlanders had taken their fill of plunder, rape and murder, they headed Southeast towards Aberdeen, sacking the countryside as they went. Their route carried them well clear of Forres and the Brodie lands, and we may imagine a sigh of relief, but all the gentry of the Northeast, including John of Brodie, took their followers and their weapons and rode to

Aberdeen for the confrontation with the Macdonald's army still remembered as *"Reid Harlaw"*

The Macdonalds had collected several other clans to join in the action and share the booty. This confederation, dominated by the Macdonalds but including Macintoshes, Macleans, Macleods and Clan Chattan bears a striking similarity to that which rose in support of the Stuarts more than three centuries later. In 1411, as in 1715, the Brodies were on the side of established order, and furiously opposed the depredations of the Highland caterans. The word *cateran* originally denoted a lightly armoured fighting man, but experience of the highlanders had changed its meaning to *barbarian*. The Macdonalds approached Aberdeen with 10,000 of them.

The Scottish historian John Major describes the clothing and equipment of the highland warriors at that time:

"... Their dress is a loose plaid and a shirt saffron dyed. They are armed with a bow and arrows, a broadsword, and a small halberd... they always carry a dagger...in time of war they wear a coat of iron rings, and in it they fight. "

The defenders, led by the Earl of Mar, fell on the highlanders in a day of red slaughter at Harlaw, near Inverurie. The Macdonald Champion, Red Hector of the Battles, was slain in single combat with the chief of the Irvines. Still the Macdonald's kept coming with the cry *"Another for Hector!"*...They were to use the same battlecry as they charged into the hail of grapeshot at Culloden. Both sides suffered dreadful losses, but eventually the highlanders withdrew and the fragile rule of law reasserted itself in Scotland. Over fifteen hundred men lay dead on the field.

And such a weary burying,

I'm sure you never saw,

As was the Sunday after that,

On the moors beneath Harlaw

The Brodie's dispensed the King's Justice on their lands throughout the fifteenth century, and answered for their decisions. John of Brodie was well known for just arbitration of disputes, and Alexander Brodie of Brodie was summoned before the Lords of Council in Edinburgh to explain one of his verdicts in 1484. Others of the family held Church livings in the area. The Brodies were a force for stability in a society that survived on the edge of chaos.

John of Brodie granted part of the revenues of his lands to Pluscarden Abbey to show repentance for *"Some rash act"* that he had committed. He was a courageous man, and a loyal one, for he once fought in a friend's battle because he happened to be passing. The friend in the case was Mackenzie of Kintail, who was at feud with the Macdonald "Lords of the Isles" over the control of the Earldom of Ross. The lands had been forfeited by Macdonald for rebellion, and bestowed on Mackenzie. He was married to a cousin of the Macdonald, Lady Margaret. She was blind in one eye. As the feud developed, Mackenzie sent Lady Margaret back to her clan, riding on a one eyed horse, accompanied by a one eyed servant, and followed by a one eyed dog.

Macdonald of Lochalsh responded to the insult by sending out the fiery cross to summon his men. He led 1800 of them into Ross, where they burned, looted and raped their way across the country. There was no force in the area strong enough to face them. They took Inverness by storm, put in their own garrison, and looted the town and the surrounding area. They despoiled the Urquhart lands around Inverness, and then travelled north to attack Strath Conan. They barricaded the women and children of the village of Contin into their church, and burned it with them trapped inside. Even by Macdonald standards, their reprisals were excessive. Eventually they made camp in a wooded valley on the Conan River, at a place called Park. It was not far from Mackenzie's home at Kinellan.

Mackenzie could raise just 600 men, but he decided to attack the Macdonalds in their camp. The night before the battle, John of Brodie arrived at Kinellan with a modest force of his clansmen as an escort. He was travelling through the area, and wanted only to stay for one night at Mackenzie's house. He was made welcome, and given a bed for the night. As he was preparing to leave the next morning he saw the Mackenzie clansmen equipped for battle, and asked, was there to be a fight today? Mackenzie told him that there was. Brodie instructed his men to make ready; he would lead them against the Macdonalds. When Mackenzie said that there was no need for the Brodies to join the unequal contest, Brodie declared that *"He would be an ill fellow and a worse neighbour that would leave his friend at such a time. "*

The Clan fighting that plagued Scotland had prepared them for what was to come. The men of Moray were skilled in the use of bow and sword, and inured to hard living. They had been raised to live in stone huts with few comforts. They had to hunt and fish for their food, and to expect battle with their neighbours. Fighting was part of their lives, usually without warning and without mercy to the loser. Their dark woollen plaids were warm and windproof even when wet, and easily adapted as a blanket for sleeping in the heather. They had few luxuries, but they had pleasure in singing and in the music of the pipes, and in the stories of battles long ago. They were courageous to a fault, proud, quarrelsome and foolhardy. They were bound to their Lairds by the system called *Kindness*, a mixture of kinship and tradition that had grown from mutual dependency, and was far stronger than written law. They travelled together to Strath Conan. Their scouts brought good news. The Macdonalds were in their camp, unaware of their approach. The wooded valley was ideal for the clansmen's stealthy approach, they surrounded the invaders without raising the alarm.

The Clansmen knew that in the melee they could distinguish friend from foe by their battle cry, and perhaps by a plant worn as a badge on the plaid. The Battle Cry in Gaelic is "Sluagh Ghairm", the origin of the word "Slogan". In battle, John of Brodie's slogan was *"A Brodie! A Brodie!"* which would identify him to his allies, and serve as a formal introduction to a very short acquaintance for his enemies. A blast from the Mackenzies hunting horn came too late to warn the Macdonalds, for they looked up to see six hundred men, with broadswords and axes raised, erupt from the woods and charge furiously down to destroy them. John of Brodie played a distinguished part in the battle, and we can imagine him in the thick of the fighting, cleaving and hacking with his great two- handed broadsword, the battle cry on his lips, scattering the foe.

Lochalsh was wounded and captured, the surviving Macdonalds fled, and the Earldom of Ross was no longer in dispute. The Battle, remembered as *Blar Na Parc*, was followed by such atrocities that the Mackenzies were themselves charged with rebellion. The Mackenzies and Macdonalds were confirmed in their feud, which was destined to last for centuries. The friendship between the Brodies and Mackenzies was also to last. The battle done, John of Brodie continued on his journey

3. FORRES, BRODIE AND DYKE

Forres is a jewel of a town. There are pavement cafes during the summer, and excellent pubs and restaurants open all year round. The mildness of the climate is amazing when you consider that the town is further North than Moscow or Labrador. In summer the sky is never fully dark, and in mid¬ winter it scarcely gets light, but the weather stays mild throughout. Some say this is the effect of the tail of the Gulf Stream, entering the Firth from round the North of Scotland, or perhaps the sheltering effect of the mountains that enclose the Laigh. Whatever the cause, it is welcome. Forres has been a Royal Borough since 1150, self-governing until 1974, sending representatives to Royal Parliaments as part of the "Three Estates" until 1707. The Royal Boroughs had privileges in trade, and administered the King's laws within their bounds, and they paid for their privileges with taxation. Only people with capital were allowed to move into the town, and they were charged startlingly high sums just to live here. These "Burgesses" shared the privileges of the town, getting first refusal on goods imported for sale, and forming comfortable Merchant Guilds that ensured that the development of trade did not bring them too much competition. Burgesses were required to keep weapons and they could be conscripted to defend the town or for Royal Service. They were also liable to pay extraordinary taxes in times of national emergency. Even so, they prospered. Each Burgess was given a plot of land called a *feu*, and he was required to build a house upon it within two years of joining the borough. At first, the feus served as small plots where a cow could be kept and a few vegetables grown, but trade prospered and did away with the need for subsistence farming within the town. So the burgesses built cottages around the edges of their plots where their employees and servants could live, and that is where the "closes" the little quadrangles of housing that make up much of the town, began. The owners gradually needed larger premises, and there was no room to build extensions, so they built upwards instead, adding up to four storeys on the same original building. Even today, you can look at the outsides of some of the buildings and make out the joins. The Town

Cross, where the ordinary folk held their unprivileged markets, was the place where proclamations were delivered. All of the great events of Scotland's history have been announced at its foot. Taxes and customs were collected at a booth, built for the purpose, and the Tollbooth gradually expanded to become the town prison and Council offices. In former times the town had its own gallows as well, and the hangman's wife had to look after the children that her husband orphaned.

The Town is picturesque, but you have to look to find evidence of its real age. So many of the "Great Men" that visited the town (The Wolf of Badenoch, Edward I, Montrose, to name but a few) left it in flames that it is surprising that it survived at all. A little way out from the centre of the town, on the road to Findhom, is a startling monument to antiquity, called Sueno's Stone. It is a sandstone column, 23 feet high, and completely covered in intricate carvings. One side is a magnificent Christian Cross, elaborately filled with Celtic Knot work. The reverse is a kind of strip cartoon of a battle. In the bottom panel, archers lead massed warriors and cavalry. In the middle panel, captives are executed, leaving a pile of headless corpses. Many of the dead lie under a bridge, thought to represent the Bridge over the Findhom 1000 years ago. One of the severed heads is framed to emphasise its importance. It may represent the death in battle of King Dubh at Forres in 967 AD. His body was missing, and the sun went black and did not reappear until it was found, hidden beneath the bridge. The tradition gains authenticity from the fact that there was a full eclipse on the 10th July, 967.

Another stone of great antiquity marks the eastern boundary of the town in Victoria Street. It is called the Witches Stone and is linked to the witch trials that stain the town's history, but it may have an older religious significance. In ancient times, stones were placed to the east of a community to catch the first rays of the sun, and libations of milk, and perhaps worse, were poured over the stone as offerings. This practice survives into modem times as spitting on the stone for luck. Today the witch's stone is remembered as marking the place where women were burned to death for witchcraft. Some were rolled down nearby Cluny hill first in barrels of nails. There were distinct periods of witch hysteria in Scotland, the last being the late seventeenth century. Between the spring of 1661 and the autumn of 1662 there were about 600 witch trials leading to 300 executions. One of the tests for witchcraft was to tie a woman's toes and thumbs together, and throw her in to water. If she floated, she was a witch. The tests were carried out locally in the small ponds used for soaking (retting) flax. In August 1661 the courts at Stitchill recorded that there had been 120 burnings, and that the retting ponds were choked with drowned bodies.

A more recent monument stands on top of the hill in Grant Park. This is a high tower, built to commemorate Admiral Nelson's final victory over the combined fleets of France and Spain in 1805. It is ornamented with emblems of the sailing navy; cannon, anchors, battle honours and a bust of the great man. The view from the top of the tower is breathtaking. To the North the deep blue of the Moray Firth and the green of Culbin Forest, with the deepest purple at the horizon, where the mountain peaks of Sutherland rise above the sea. To the West lush farm and woodland, with Brodie nestling among the trees. The silver thread of Findhom sparkles in the green. This leads the eye back to the Altyre and Damaway forests and the undulating hills of Braemoray with their shawl of heather.

Those hills were home to Clan Chattan, a confederation of sixteen small clans that were traditionally led by the Clan Mackintosh. They had a long power struggle with the Cummings, the descendants of the Comyns, for control of the hills. Their feuding caused so much trouble that the King eventually ordered them to fight it out in a public spectacle, thirty men a side, to the death. They were each allowed a bow, three arrows, a sword or axe, and a dirk. Their only defence was the small round leather shield, the Targe. The contest was held in a field on the North Inch of Perth, and attracted a huge crowd of spectators. Pipers played martial music, bets were laid, and the gladiators marched on to the field. They stripped to their shirts and formed up in two lines, watching each other across the sward while the crowd heckled and cheered. When the King gave the signal both sides fired off their arrows, and charged. The spectacle of sixty brawny lads butchering each other fairly delighted the crowd, who cheered themselves hoarse. When the dust had settled there were eleven wounded Mackintosh men and one dying Cumming left, so the Clan

Chattan won the day.

It did not stop the feud. From the top of Grant tower, you can just see the shell of Rait Castle to the South west. The Cummings of Rait invited the Mackintosh men to a reconciliation feast there, intending to kill them after dinner. The Mackintosh knew what was afoot, having been warned by Cummings daughter, and his men struck first; each man plunging his knife into his neighbour, rather than his dinner. The dying Cumming chief dragged himself up to his daughter's room, and found her dangling from the window ledge, trying to get out. He drew his sword and chopped her hands off at the wrist. The castle has stood empty ever since.

This routine butchery, sometimes formalised into an entertainment and patronised by the King, is symbolic of the times. Central authority was weak, anarchy reigned, and each of the great names of Scotland fought against the other for territory and status. The Crown had fewer men, less money, and less authority, than many of the magnates, and so was obliged to play one off against the other to maintain control. In the North east, the Gordons, led by the Earls of Huntly, were the dominant force. In the west the Campbells, led by the Duke of Argyll. The Brodie lands placed them squarely between the two. Clan Chattan treated the Laigh as a convenient source of supplies, and raided incessantly. Sometimes their raids went too far, as in 1531, when they burned out the Oglivie castle at Petty, killing eighteen of the garrison. There was some dispute about the Oglivie having custody of young Lachlan, the child heir of Mackintosh.

They followed up with an attack on Darnaway Castle. Unable to take it, they laid waste the parish of Dyke, burning the "whole houses" of the parish, which presumably included Brodie. Destroying the poor folk's houses was bad enough, but at that time a house could be rebuilt from natural materials within a few days if the occupants survived. The real problem came from the destruction or theft of standing crops and stored meal, and the theft of cattle on which the local economy depended. The cattle thief condemned whole communities to poverty; in a severe winter they might doom families to death by starvation. Huntly reacted vigorously. He arrested eighteen leaders of Clan Chattan, and had them put to death. He captured William, the brother of Hector, the chief. He was hanged, drawn and quartered. William's head was affixed to the cross at Dyke and his four quarters displayed at Forres, Auldearn, Inverness and Elgin. It is said that two hundred Clan Chattan men were offered their lives in exchange for information about Hectors whereabouts. One by one, they chose death before betrayal, and received it.

Perhaps the only thing that could unite the Clans was a foreign aggressor. In 1547 Henry VIII of England had decided that the toddler who was to become known as Mary, Queen of Scots, should be married to his son. His determination, remembered as *The Rough Wooing*, included sending armies into Scotland to harry and destroy, and to attempt to capture the four year old heiress. The Earl of Arran ordered the raising of the Clans to fight the aggressor. One Mungo Stratheme, whose name suggests that he came from the Nairn valley, rode through the Laigh with the fiery cross, and local feuds had to be suspended while national war was prepared. Thomas, the 11th Thane of Brodie, was to travel south with his followers as part of the Earl of Huntly's forces. We can imagine the human side of the preparations for war. How Thomas' wife, Agnes Schaw, must have worried as she packed his clothes for the journey, how Thomas must have counted, checked and rechecked the arms and equipment of his men. How painstakingly chain mail, claymores, spears and axes must have been examined, though to be sure they would not have been blunt or rusty at any time in those turbulent days. Still, there would be time to bring each weapon to a shaving edge and stow it carefully, ready for use. There would be calculations for supplies for the journey, speculation on how long it would take to engage the English, and reassurances to those staying behind that the outcome was assured, and all would return safely. The Brodies neighbours were similarly preparing. Rose of Kilravock and Hay of Lochloy, Falconer of Lethen, the Cuthberts of Castlehill were all joining Huntly for the journey south, and bringing their followers with them. We can imagine Thomas and his kin marching south with the Gordons, the pipes playing, harness jingling on the few stocky little ponies, iron glinting in the soft light of autumn. They came in time to the field of Pinkie Cleugh, where 36,000 Scots had gathered to face the English Invader.

They drew up on a ridge called Edmonstone Edge, behind the town of Musselburgh. Huntly rode among them, splendid in plate armour that was enamelled and gilt edged to sparkle in the sunlight. Black robed priests took mass on the open hillside, blessing the Scots in their fight. Below the hill, across the River Esk, the English Army was drawn up. They gleamed like a new tapestry with tents and banners fluttering in the wind, plate armour and steel tipped lances catching the sun among the numberless barded horses, great guns being dragged into position. Beyond them, in the Firth, English warships and transports lay at anchor with their rows of cannon facing the shore. A galley ran swiftly between them with its banks of oars beating like the wings of a bird. Regiments of harquebusiers (musketeers), some on horseback, were deployed to cover the river crossings. A great host of foot soldiers armed with pikes formed a wall across the field. Many of them were Spanish and Portuguese mercenaries, who had a reputation for torturing prisoners to death.

The English host was not well led. All the tactical lessons of Anglo/Scots conflict were ignored as the English cavalry deployed to charge uphill against prepared Scottish positions. English observers saw the Scots spears *"as thick as the spines of a hedgehog"* but no archers or guns were deployed to break them up. Instead the cavalry hurled itself against the spears in a mighty thundering wave, and like a wave upon a rock they broke and spilled, the edges going around and the centre crashing into ruin. Fallen riders tried to rise and penetrate the wall, and were spitted on spears or cut down by a hail of arrows and sling stones. Their momentum broken, the remaining riders rode at the edge of the formations, trying to find a way past the wall of spears, but there was no way. They turned and rode back down the hill... and the Scots followed.

Arran, Huntly, Brodie and all the Scots leaders must have seen the danger and tried to call their men back. But the Scots had put their enemy to flight, their blood was up and the downhill charge had begun. They charged as individuals, scattered incoherently across the hillside. They charged into prepared positions and a storm of gunfire and arrows. They were scattered and spread, and the regrouped English cavalry turned and rode into them like a thunderbolt. Arran fled "with scant honour" and left his army to its fate. The Thane of Brodie was slain on the field. We may imagine a muttered prayer to Saint Jude of the Lost Causes as he saw the massed English cavalry turning towards his shattered position. Perhaps he roared out the ancient battlecry as he met them. Perhaps his kin surrounded him, and they fought and died together. Only his name, as a man of rank, was recorded among the slain.

Fourteen thousand Scots died on the field of Pinkie. The Cuthberts of Castlehill were among the slain, and Huntly and Kilravock were among the prisoners. Kilravock was released after ransom, and Huntly escaped a year after the battle. He was made Earl of Moray as a reward for his services. The English set up a chain of forts about Edinburgh, and proceeded to waste the countryside. They were unable to capture the little queen, and she was taken into hiding and then smuggled away to France. There she grew up in the French court and was married, aged fifteen, to the Dauphin. Before her wedding she signed a sheaf of documents that handed the throne of Scotland to the King of France and his successors.

When word of the disaster at Pinkie came to Brodie, Alexander became the 12th Thane. He seems to have been a wild one, "put to the horn" (outlawed as a rebel) in 1552. He was deeply involved in a blood feud between his powerful neighbour, Alexander Dunbar, the Sheriff of Elgin and Forres, and the Cummings of Altyre, the descendants of the hated Comyns. According to the charge sheet, Alexander had ridden out with Dunbar, Hay of Lochloy, Grant of Ballindalloch and one hundred and twenty six followers, to attack the house at Altyre. Their footmen were equipped for war, *"and they themselves on horse, by way of plain battle."* They broke down the gates, and put the Cummings to flight after a short skirmish *"masterfully setting upon the said Alexander Cumming and his servants, and chasing of him and them for their slaughter."* One Alistair Adamson, a Fletcher, was mutilated in the skirmish. The attackers refused to attend court to answer for this crime, which led to them being declared rebels. Alexander seems to have defied the consequences of his outlawry, for he was pardoned a year later. In 1553 he was married to Marjorie Dunbar of Durris. She bore him a son and heir, David, the thirteenth Thane.

This connection to the Dunbars drew Alexander deeper into his alliance with the Sheriff. During 1553 Lord Arran (who had fled the field of Pinkie where Brodie's father had died) made a ruling intended to end the feud. He said that Dunbar and Cumming *"for the revenging of old deadly feuds...make continual and daily gatherings of their kin...whereby the whole country and bounds adjacent thereto is in readiness to break..."* Arran's solution was that each of the contenders should give his eldest son into the keeping of Huntly, as a hostage against their future good behaviour. He also authorised Huntly, as Lieutenant of the North, to raise the common army of the Scots to enforce the ruling. Patrick Dunbar did not go into Huntly's keeping. He went out with his father, and Alexander Brodie, Hay of Lochloy, and about fifty others, and attacked Cumming again. This time they killed his son, two of his kinsmen, and three of his servants. Once again, they refused to attend the court in Edinburgh to answer for their actions. Once again, they were "Put to the Horn" as rebels and outlaws. Their moveable property, land, rents, *"sums of money, jewels, gold, silver... and other goods whatsoever"* were to be given to the Church, in the earthly form of the Prior of Pluscarden and the Dean of Moray, who happened to be a Dunbar. The Brodies had lost Brodie...in theory. This notional transfer of assets needed military power to enforce, which the Church did not possess. Huntly had bigger fish to fry, and he needed allies. The common army of the Scots was not raised. The Church was in more danger, in 1550's Moray, than Brodie or his colleagues.

Alexander was outlawed during the time of the Scottish Reformation. Public opinion was pushing the country towards the Protestant reformed religion. The Bible had been translated into English, and printed copies were becoming available everywhere. Many people were convinced that they could understand their creed without need of priests. The Church itself was seen as corrupt and hypocritical, with good reason. The monks of Pluscarden scandalised the neighbourhood with their debauched lifestyle, and the Priory was eventually forced to close. The monks of Kinloss lived like gentlemen, with servants to wait on them and concubines in residence. The Bishop of Moray lived like a lord in Spynie Castle, defying Catholic and Protestant principles alike. When the reformation came he married his mistress in Elgin Cathedral and gave his troop of illegitimate children estates out of Church lands. The church was the richest institution in the country, wealthier than the Crown and Magnates combined. When the Reformation came, in 1560, it brought a redistribution of Church property. The Brodies eventually gained some land in Dyke, and a field called the Stable Acre, formerly the property of the Bishop.

Huntly did not accept the Reformation. He had no rival for wealth and power in the North east, and is still remembered as *the Cock o' the North*. He would have no part of the religious revolution, and the Gordons remained Catholic. He even conspired to bring the Queen back from France as a figurehead for a Catholic counter-revolution, using his power and her right to sweep the reformers away. She declined his offer gracefully. The Stewarts and the Campbells were enthusiastic reformers, and a new element was added to the rivalries of the magnates. Then, in 1561, the Queen came back.

Mary, Queen of Scots, was just eighteen years old and strikingly beautiful. She was also the widow of the French King, heir apparent to the throne of England and a devout Catholic. She was a gifted horsewoman, dancer and poet. Her subjects loved her, but the newly established Protestant Kirk, led by a murderous bigot called John Knox, denounced her as a witch and a whore. Knox bellowed from the pulpit that one mass said in Scotland would do more damage than ten thousand enemy soldiers. Knox tried to forbid Mary from attending mass, even in her private chambers. Her French servants were assaulted and her priests went in fear of their lives. Mary compromised her religious beliefs in a naive bid to win the co¬ operation of the Kirk, even acceding to the persecution of her Catholic subjects. This was too much for Huntly. He believed the Queen to be virtually a prisoner of the Protestant faction. He wanted to marry her to his son. Sir John Gordon, and return Scotland to Catholicism at the point of a sword. He was ready to make war on his sovereign, and Alexander Brodie was ready to join him, as part of his old alliance with the Dunbars and the Hays.

Mary came to the Laigh of Moray in September 1562. Her natural brother, James Stewart, and the flower of Scotland's nobility accompanied her. They made as villainous a crew as had ever been assembled to escort a pretty girl. Throughout the Royal progress a large force of armed men led by Huntly in person shadowed them. They spent two days at Kinloss Abbey, which clearly still had the means to entertain royally, then travelled to Darnaway Castle. Both Dunbar and Huntly had once held Darnaway as Earls of Moray, and it must have galled them to see the symbol of power in Morayshire occupied by the Queen and her heretic court. She held a State Council there, in the great hall built by Earl Randolph. There she invested her brother James Stewart with the Earldom of Moray. This poisoned gift, Huntly's former title, made Stewart one of the most powerful men in the land, and the custodian of all the Royal castles in the North. Mary left a gift of her own embroidery at Darnaway, which may still be seen in the hall. She dined at Moyness Castle, on the Muckle Burn, and then continued her journey to Inverness. There she demanded entrance to her Castle, and was refused. Sir John Gordon, Huntly's son, had given orders to his Gordons in the garrison that she was not to be admitted. Mary slept that night in a private house in Inverness, but her brother James was busy.

The Queen awoke the next morning to find the men of the Frasers, Munroes and Clan Chattan, armed and ready to storm the castle. Mary was in high spirits, wishing that she were a man to take a broadsword and buckler, and join them. As they formed up to attack, the Gordon commander had a change of heart, and surrendered. Huntly had sent word that the Queen was to be admitted, and presented with the keys to the Castle. Mary went in, and had the Gordon commander summarily tried for treason and hanged from the castle gate. The Queen stayed at Inverness for four days, and then travelled back to Aberdeen via Kilravock and Darnaway. Once back in Aberdeen, she declared Huntly an outlaw, and forfeited him of all rank and privilege, even to confiscating his own castle at Strathbogie. He responded by marching towards Aberdeen with eight hundred men.

This final act of rebellion was suicidal. Huntly should have been able to field twenty thousand fighting men, but few wished to take arms against their sovereign, whatever their Clan loyalties. Young Lachlan Mackintosh had sent word to prevent his Clan Chattan men from joining the Gordon standard, and no doubt they did some further preventing on their own initiative. Why the Brodie joined in with Huntly's desperate gamble can never be known. Perhaps it was religious conviction that drove him, perhaps loyalty to his Hay and Dunbar kin, and to the man who had commanded the left wing at Pinkie, where Brodie's father fell. Perhaps it was an ingrained determination to see a fight through to the finish, regardless of the odds. Whatever the reason, it brought the Brodie clansmen to the Hill of Fare, and the odds were three to one against.

The Hill is a high granite outcrop, about fifteen miles west of Aberdeen. From their position on the hillside they could see the Queen's forces, vastly superior in numbers but less well positioned. Huntly knew that many of them were his feudal subjects and co¬ religionists, and he did not believe they would fight. Huntly was an old, corpulent, dour man with a history of extreme violence. Faced with this crisis, he had sworn to heaven that he would reform if God gave him the victory. Paradoxically, his plan was to defeat the Queen's forces and then storm Aberdeen to seize her person, no doubt reforming soon after. Huntly believed his confidence to be well founded. His wife had consulted a seer, who had revealed that Huntly would lie that night in the Aberdeen Tollbooth, with never a wound upon him.

The Queen's men, led by the new Earl of Moray, did not storm the hill. They positioned one hundred and twenty Harquebusiers (musketeers) and kept up a hail of fire that made the hillside untenable. The rebels scrambled downhill alongside of a pretty brook, the "Bonny Burn" of Corrichie. Attempting to charge, they found themselves in the marsh fed by the burn, with the stream behind them and their numerically superior opponents pressing them down. A desperate struggle followed at push of pike, a grim, hacking slaughter that could only have one end. Over two hundred rebels were killed, another one hundred and twenty captured. Among the prisoners were Huntly and Sir John Gordon, the Queen's erstwhile suitor. The Brodie managed to escape from the battlefield and return home, where being a rebel and outlaw did not mean he would be friendless. Huntly was led on horseback to be shown to the new Earl of Moray, a humiliation that was more than the old warrior could bear. He was seized with a stroke, and crashed down from the horse, dead before reaching the ground. He lay that night in the Aberdeen Tollbooth, with never a wound upon him.

The Earl's dead body was later propped up in court and tried for treason. This curious legal formality remained from the days of trial by combat, when the verdict of the court was given after the execution of it. Sir John and five other Gordon leaders were condemned to die, five by hanging but Sir John by beheading, as befitted his rank. Alexander was put to the horn once more, and was to spend the next four years as a hunted fugitive. The estates of Brodie were forfeit to the Crown, and the family dispossessed. A lament for the dead of Corrichie still survives:

Mourn ye highlands, mourn ye lowlands, I trow ye hae meickle need,

For the bonny burn o' Corrichie

Has run this day wi' bluid

I wish our Queen had better friends

I wish our country better peace

I wish our lords would nae discord

I wish our wars at home may cease

Queen Mary watched from a window in the tollbooth as her former suitor was beheaded. She had intended to demonstrate her remorseless fury at his treason, but the blade was blunt, the execution botched in a ghastly manner, and she had to be helped from the room. The Maiden, a Scottish variant of the guillotine on which Sir John Gordon died, may still be seen in the Town house in Aberdeen. There is a monument to the battlefield of Corrichie at the Hill of Fare, about fifteen miles west of Aberdeen, near the B977 south west of Garlogie village. The area is now heavily wooded, but it is possible to follow the burn back to the hill. There is a dell near the field where Mary is said to have watched the battle.

Poor Mary, Queen of Scots. All the courts of Europe wooed her, but she tried to stand by her small, impoverished, violent homeland and it took her life. She married for love, not power, and her husband Damley proved as treacherous and murderous as the rest of the Scots Lords. Four years after the battle of Corrichie she needed allies. To gain them, she released the surviving son of the Earl of Huntly from prison, and pardoned Alexander Brodie. He returned to his restored estate at the beginning of the period of bloodshed, treachery and murder that was to lead the young queen to the executioner's block.

In 1567 Mary's husband was murdered and she was abducted, raped and forced to marry the principal murderer, Bothwell. The scandal led to her abdication and flight into England, where she was promptly imprisoned by Elizabeth I. Scotland had a child King again, the infant James VI, and the magnates began fighting for control. James Stewart, the Queen's half brother became Regent of Scotland. Brodie began improving the defences of his fortified house.

The keep was built to the established North Eastern design. High, straight walls with battlements and enclosed towers at opposite comers, allowing a clear field of fire to all four sides. Access only at first floor level, with arrow slits and gun loops commanding the approaches to the house. Spiral staircases leading down to the ground floor kitchens and up to the laird's apartments. The entrance opened into the high hall (now the red drawing room) where the laird kept his table in front of the great fireplace. It was practical, comfortable in the Spartan fashion of the time, and eminently defensible.

The local wars made fortification a necessity, even for a private house. Sheriff Dunbar, pardoned for his part in Huntly's rebellion, was now fighting a deadly feud with the family of Innes. Both sides were condemned *"for greatly perturbing the public peace and committing cruel slaughter..."* in proclamations read at the market cross. The Regent Moray, ruling on behalf of the infant King, tried to put the Sheriff to useful work. He ordered him to have the lead roof of Elgin Cathedral removed and sold. The reformation had made "The Lantern of the North" a symbol of Catholicism, and it suited public policy to have it degraded. The lead was loaded into two ships, which foundered in a storm at sea, so the Regent did not profit by his vandalism. A paid assassin killed Moray barely two years after his appointment. Mary, still in prison in England, rewarded her brother's killer with a small pension. Moray's successor, Lennox, was killed the following year, and his successor. Mar, died suddenly fourteen months later. He had just finished eating supper with one of his rivals for the regency. A Convention was called to elect a new Regent, and Alexander Brodie was chosen to be one of the electors.

They met in Edinburgh in November 1572. The great castle was still held by supporters of the exiled Queen and besieged by English and foreign troops. Supporters of the Regency, who claimed allegiance to the infant King, held the town. A mutual desultory artillery bombardment was steadily reducing both to rubble. There was little fuel and less food for the common folk. Alexander had spent much of his adult life resisting the authority of his country's capital, but he could have taken no pleasure in its ruin. The convention of Earls, Bishops, Lords and Barons met in the midst of this chaos to choose their new leader. The electors had written to the Earl Morton, the host of Regent Mar's last supper, to ask if he would obey the decision of the convention. He assured them that he would. In the end they made it easy for him, by electing him Regent.

Alexander returned to find business as usual in the Burgh of Forres. A party of Sheriff Dunbar's men had hampered an election of Burgh officials. Dunbar had positioned them, dressed in full war gear, at the Tollbooth to refuse admission to the electors. The Sheriff then announced that he had chosen the officials, he would be Provost, and an election would not be necessary. The electors withdrew to the house of Urquhart of Burdsyards, and held their election. They chose Urquhart as Provost, perhaps because his house was "The only sure place" they could convene. Dunbar would not allow them to take up their duties, and even shot one of Urquhart's servants and imprisoned two burgh officials, one of whom was called Andrew Brodie. The electors complained directly to the Regent, professing their loyalty and Dunbar's open rebellion. This seems to have had effect, as Dunbar was 'Put to the Horn' soon after. Surprisingly, Andrew Brodie was outlawed in the same proclamation. His home at Golfurd, on the Border of the Brodie and Dunbar lands, may have made co-operation with the outlaw Sheriff seem wise. In the following year the Dunbars attacked Urquhart's lands, stealing horses, cattle and stacked crops. The prior of Pluscarden made the complaint against him, for depriving the local ministers of their subsistence.

Alexander married twice during his turbulent life. His first wife was

Marjory Dunbar, the mother of David, the 13th Thane. He married again in 1569 to Margaret Hay, the widow of Dunbar of Bengafield. She was the daughter of Hay of Lochloy, Brodie's ally in the feuds and battles of the 1550's. Between them they had twelve children, David, the 13th Brodie, six Dunbar boys and five Brodie girls. When Alexander died, in 1583, the Dunbars attempted to disinherit David in favour of the oldest son of her first marriage. They did not succeed. David was 30 years old when he became the 13th Brodie of Brodie. The Laigh was still an extremely dangerous place. The slow burning feud between the Stewart Earls of Moray and Huntly's Gordons occasionally burst into violence. The Roses of Kilravock and the Dunbars were fighting a steadily escalating land war, and importing broken clansmen from the highlands to strengthen their forces. Clan Chattan continued to raid the farmlands of the Laigh, although a succession of severe winters and wet summers had impoverished the people. Everyone went armed with a sword and dagger, and a loaded pistol in the belt was considered an item of high fashion.

In 1584 David was married to Janet Hay, the youngest daughter of Hay of Lochloy and his stepmothers younger sister. The only glimpses we have of them are in the legal records of the Privy Council. These show that David continued his fathers feud with the Cummings of Altyre, and may have conspired with Huntly in supporting the Spanish attempt at the invasion of Britain. There is no positive proof of this, just the conspicuous absence of David's signature from a declaration of loyalty to the King and enmity to Huntly that was drawn up in 1589. In this document the names of blood feud enemies are found side by side in support of the King's cause. Patrick Dunbar, Cumming of Altyre, Campbell of Cawdor, Hay of Lochloy, Rose of Kilravock, Kinnaird of Culbin...but not Brodie of Brodie. Huntly was caught offering armed support to the Spaniards. He wanted the Armada to land on the Moray coast, where ten thousand Gordon swords would have helped the Duke of Parma to conquer Britain. Queen Elizabeth of England was furious, but James VI of Scotland was not, and Huntly did not really suffer for his treason. King James was inordinately fond of the rebellious earl and always found reason to excuse his treachery. He even connived with Huntly in the murder of one of his own Stewart Kinsmen, in the almost legendary events recalled in the folk song "The Bonny Earl of Moray."

Ye Highlands and ye lowlands, Oh where ha 'e ye bin

They hae slain the Earl o' Murray

And laid him on the green

Now woe to thee Huntly, and wherefore did ye say,

I bade you bring him to me but forbade ye him to slay

He was a braw gallant And he rode at the ring

And the Bonny Earl o' Murray, he might have been a king

Oh long will his lady,

Look frae the Castle Doune

Ee 'r she see the Earl o' Murray

Come sounding through the town

The "Bonny Earl" ruled a comparatively small area of Morayshire, sandwiched between the massive power blocks of Huntly's Gordons and Argyll's Campbells. His Earldom had been forfeited by Huntly for one of his earlier rebellions, but the Gordon continued to collect rents and fishing rights that should have been the Stewart's. This led to armed conflict and the familiar toll of destruction of crops and cattle for the working people of the Laigh. Even the fishermen's boats on the Spey were deliberately destroyed. All of the Northern Clans became aligned, including the Campbells under Campbell of Cawdor, who welcomed Moray's attempts to bring down his Gordon enemy. The Clan leaders met in Forres to formalise their alliance, Cawdor and Dunbar, Mackintosh for Clan Chattan, Grant of Freuchie for the Speyside Grants, Fraser of Lovat and others. Patrick Dunbar, Brodie's old ally and kinsman, supported Moray but argued that it was futile to oppose Huntly "in these parts." He refused to sign a pact of mutual assistance. While the anti-Gordon alliance wrangled, Huntly was on the move. He had heard of the meeting, and rapidly assembled several hundred armed men to break it up. Hearing of his approach, the Clan leaders withdrew, Moray himself returning to his castle at Darnaway. Huntly followed him there, and the two sides exchanged fire. John Gordon, Huntly's friend and kinsman, fell dead from his horse, shot through the mouth. Huntly's rage knew no bounds.

What followed seems more like a civil war than the sporadic clashes of everyday blood feuding. Moray assembled an army at Forres, and used them to harry the borders of the Gordon lands. Moray's men repeatedly attacked Culbin, although Kinnaird had signed the anti-Huntly bond only a year or two earlier. Huntly fortified Elgin Cathedral and the old bishop's palace at Spynie, filled the town with his Gordon fighting men, and brought in fifty "Gentlemen" at arms, with two horses apiece, as his cavalry. The Clansmen looted the surrounding countryside indiscriminately, but they did not meet in open battle. The King ordered Huntly to withdraw his forces to the East of the Spey, and Moray's men to the West of the Findhorn. Cross-river raiding in both directions tormented the inhabitants of the Laigh, with literally hundreds of men killed and thousands of animals slaughtered or stolen. Two cooks were burned alive by Huntly, who sent word to his enemies that he had left two roasts for them. The violence even spread abroad, where children at school in France, relatives of Huntly's, were sought out and murdered by Moray's men. Even so, the Gordons had the best of it, and Moray's support began to fall away. The Grants and Clan Chattan changed sides to become Huntly's men again. Only the threat of Campbell reprisals prevented Huntly from invading and sweeping all before him. Moray was isolated and facing ruin. Then the King intervened, with an offer of arbitration.

A letter from the court brought Moray to his mother's farm on the coast at Donibristle, to await the King's summons. Patrick Dunbar travelled with him. The Sherriff had tried to stop Moray from attacking Huntly from the start, but he was still at his side at the end. They did not know, as they awaited the King's word in the thatched farm buildings, that Campbell of Cawdor had just been shot dead by Huntly's assassins, and that the new Campbell leader was sworn to the Gordon. They did not know that the King's arbitration was a ruse, and that Huntly was on his way to Donibristle with eighty well armed mounted men. The King had even ordered the ferries across the Forth to be suspended after Huntly had crossed, to prevent the Bonny Earl's friends from warning him. Moray had only twelve men with him, on that cold February afternoon, and the farm at Donibristle had no defences at all.

The fight was short and bitter. Huntly sent Captain John Gordon forward to demand the Earls surrender, and he was immediately shot down. Soon after, the thatch was fired. Huntly's men surrounded the burning building, picking off the defenders by the light of the flames. Patrick Dunbar knew how to weigh the odds, and he knew that they could not hold out for long. He volunteered to create a diversion to cover the Earl's escape. Moray would escape from the back of the building. Dunbar would leave the building by the front door, and attack Huntly's men, who would believe him to be the Earl. As Moray slipped away, the Sherriff charged alone from out of the blazing farm, roaring his defiance and slashing right and left until he was brought down. So died Patrick Dunbar, a fitting and honourable end to a notable man. May Holy Saint Jude of the Lost Causes cast incense on his name. Huntly and his men soon found Moray hiding on the shore, and they hacked him to death. With the last of his strength he told Huntly that he had *"Spoiled a bonnier face than his own."* The murder did not end the feud. Moray's mother refused to allow the Earl to be buried until justice had been done, and both Huntly and the King dissembled in the face of outraged public opinion. Years more of repetitive bloodshed and strife followed, finally settled by the arranged marriages of Huntly's heir to Argyll's daughter and Moray's to Huntly's daughter Anne. They toasted each other kindly at their wedding feasts, and ignored the bitter rivalries that had cost a thousand lives. A portrait of the Bonny Earl, displaying his death wounds, hangs today in Darnaway Castle. A scroll issues from his mouth forming the words *"God Revenge My Cause".* It is framed with timber from the gallows on which a couple of unfortunate Gordon scapegoats were hanged. It is said that James VI refused even to look at it.

Where was David, the thirteenth Thane, while all this was going on?. Well, he was in the thick of it. Sandwiched between Moyness,

Darnaway, Cawdor and Culbin, he could not have hoped to stay neutral. George Bain's classic 1893 History of Nairnshire states that David sided with Huntly, although he gives no sources for the statement. We have seen that he refused to condemn Huntly in 1589. Then again, he had fought alongside the Dunbars in numerous smaller fights, and was to do so again, joining them in their battle with the Roses in the years after Morays death. He was, after all, a Dunbar on his mother's side, and the 12th Thane had ridden into battle with Patrick Dunbar while David was still a child. Then again, the Dunbars had tried to disinherit him, and he would not have forgotten that in a hurry. David's story burned with Brodie in 1645, and perhaps it is just as well. There were no good guys in the bloodfeud days. Courageous, treacherous, lightning- quick with sword and dagger, tireless in revenge, David not only survived the bloodfeud days, he thrived in them. He and Janet had seven sons, and they all inherited fine estates. David, the eldest, became the 14th Thane of Brodie, and the other six founded landed branches of the family, including Alexander, the 1st Brodie of Lethen. Their third son, John, became Dean of Moray and their youngest, Joseph, became the Presbyterian Minister of Forres. David himself was cautioned from time to time to stop going after the Cummings and picking on the Roses, but he lived to be 73 years old, a remarkable age for his time and place.

We get a glimpse of David in the records of the Wapinschaw (weapon - show) of 1596, when James VI ordered the men of Moray to assemble in arms at Kilravock. Although James was Heir Apparent to the Throne of England, he suspected that he would have to conquer his new kingdom when Elizabeth I died. He held musters throughout the country to prepare, and once more the feuding had to be suspended while the Clans made ready for war. They assembled at Kilravock on a cold February morning, five years after the death of the Bonny Earl. The Dunbars, the Cummings of Altyre, the Kinnairds of Culbin, the Hays of Lochloy. All were mounted and clad in their best armour, ready for war. We may imagine how they looked at each other. Brodie and Hay rode to the muster together, and David is recorded as being: *"On horse, with Jack, steel bonnet, plate sleeves, hagbutt (gun), spear and sword...the said David Brodie specified to serve his majesty within or without the country... "* David was equally willing to attack his neighbours or to invade England.

It is said that when King James VI of Scotland visited Morayshire, he asked Rose of Kilravock how he had managed to reach a ripe old age among such troublesome neighbours. Kilravock replied that they were the best neighbours a man could have, as they made him get down on his knees and pray three times a day, when he might otherwise not have prayed at all. The Brodies certainly played their part in maintaining the piety of the Laigh of Moray throughout the 16th Century.

4. AULDEARN, LETHEN,ELGIN

The route that Mary, Queen of Scots took on her journey from Darnaway to Inverness still exists, though it is no longer the main road. These days the A96 trunk road carries fast traffic from Inverness to Elgin and Aberdeen. It branches away from the original route and skirts past Auldearn to the North. I dare say most drivers don't notice the village. It is a small place, very old, and long ago it was strategically significant. The road that runs through the village used to be guarded by a royal castle. The Castle was called Eren, and 'Auld Eren' became Auldearn. William the Lion, who gave Scotland its Lion banner, held court here. Robert the Bruce received the surrender of the Earl of Ross within Old Eren's walls. Only traces of the foundations remain today. Looking eastwards we see Auldearn Church, rebuilt in 1757 but still incorporating some of the walls, and many of the features, of its ancient predecessor. There is a carved funeral inscription to Hay of Lochloy, the father in law and ally of both Alexander and David during the bloodfeud days, buried here in 1563. Loch Loy today is a small lake at the eastern end of the Culbin forest, but old maps seem to show that it was once an inlet of the sea. The Hays had their castle at Inshoch ("The Island Field"), an imposing affair with a Z plan keep, built around the same time as Brodie. The Island shows as a mound among the flat and level farmlands that used to be marsh. A Hay coat of arms recovered from the ruins may still be seen, built into the gable wall of Inshoch farm. The Brodie's acquired the Hay lands in 1695.

Another of the tombs in Auldearn Church is the family vault of the Brodies of Lethen. This is a fine estate on the Muckle Burn, just south of Moyness. The Falconer family, who have an ancient memorial in Auldearn Church, originally held it. They suffered badly during the feuding years, and sold their estate to the Grants, who sold it to

Alexander, the brother of the 14th Thane, in 1634. Alexander, a puritan, prospered as a burgess of Edinburgh, and had a successful banking business. He paid £7,500 for Lethen, an astronomical sum in those days. He also suffered enormous financial losses during the Civil War, but still managed to expand his estates. By 1643 he was able to buy the old Abbey lands of Kinloss, and he eventually held more land than his nephew, the Brodie.

There is a Dunbar family tomb in Auldearn Church, as well, the last home of the Dunbars of Boath. They built the picturesque seventeenth century circular dovecote, that still stands among the remains of Old Eren. Dovecotes used to be a symbol of conspicuous wealth, only those with land enough to feed the birds were allowed to build them. The Dunbars had Boath House and its lands, so there was no problem with birdseed. They acquired the place in 1555, during the bloodfeud years, and this is one of the puzzling things about our story. How is it that our ancestors ravaged and wasted this countryside for generations, were repeatedly outlawed and forfeited, and still increased their wealth? Rents were generally set as a proportion of the produce of the tenant. Over and again we hear of land and crops burned, tenants butchered, animals killed or driven off, a systematic destruction of the economic base. Yet they still prospered. Alexander and David must have been able to defend their own property and seize their neighbours. Some of the herds driven off the Moray lands during the feud must have found their way to Brodie, and then to market. The Brodie lands were a forward position for Huntly, being West of the Findhorn and close to Darnaway. We hear of Culbin being repeatedly attacked by Moray's men, but not Brodie. Perhaps it was too tough a nut to crack.

The second David, the 14th Thane, was born in 1586. In 1613 he married Catherine Dunbar, a daughter of the Bishop of Moray and the niece of The Admirable Crichton, a remarkable character in Scottish history. Crichton was a handsome and dashing youth, of astonishing intellect. At 17 he could debate philosophy, science and mathematics in ten different languages with the leading professors of the age. He was an expert horseman, skilled in jousting and swordplay. He was a famous duellist, poet, and ladies man. In the 1580's he went abroad. After many

European adventures he was made tutor to Vincenzo, an ungovernable Italian Prince. One night the youth attacked him in the street. Crichton could have killed the Prince, but chose instead to give him his own sword as a gesture of trust. Vincenzo ran him through with it. So died the Admirable Crichton, aged 22, of naivety. It wouldn't have happened to his Morayshire in-laws

David and Catherine had seven children, four boys and three girls. In 1620 they dealt with a neighbour dispute, with Dunbar of Grangehill, by taking him to court and getting him fined. This shows that the times really were changing, and that the courts were becoming a genuine alternative to armed intervention in a local dispute. The Presbyteries were very earnest about stopping the deadly feuds, and as their influence grew the levels of local violence sensibly diminished. One witness to the changes was John Wyland, the Steward at Brodie, who served the 13th, 14th and 15th Thanes, faithful to the end of his days. David and Catherine's first-born son was named Alexander, and he was destined to become the most famous of all the Brodies of Brodie.

Alexander was born in 1617, at the beginning of a new kind of turbulence for the Laigh. The blood feuds of the last age had not yet ended. The Gordons were making war on the Mackintoshes, seeking to drive them out of the county. The Reformation had taken root, but a long and violent struggle between the Episcopalian and Presbyterian forms of the Protestant religion had begun. The common people seem to have favoured the more democratic Presbyterian forms, and were easily persuaded to Puritanism. King James preffered Episcopalian forms, and found the rule of Bishops selected by him to be convenient. James had a brutally simple view of his divine right, as King, to dictate his subject's religion.

Poverty fuelled religious intolerance. Wages in Scotland were half those of England, and emigration was an accepted way of dealing with surplus population. Thousands of Scots were serving in continental wars, and "idle and masterless men" were liable to be arrested and shipped out for military service whether they wanted to go or not. A new colony, Nova Scotia, was begun to counter the French settlement in Canada. Sir Robert Gordon of Gordonstoun was made a Baronet of Nova Scotia, suggesting that a new aristocracy might be founded by the conquest of the Americas. Thank heaven that it wasn't.

It was about this time that Shakespeare visited Forres, certainly in imagination and possibly in person. Shakespeare wrote "Macbeth " at the behest of King James VI of Scotland, who was by now King James I of England, too. He wanted to improve his image (his new subjects called him the Scotch Monkey). Shakespeare humoured James by creating Banquo, as a fictitious link between the Stuarts and the Celtic monarchy, and by portraying Lady Macbeth as the true villain of the piece. James hated women. There is no record of Shakespeare travelling the area himself, yet his local knowledge is very precise. Early folio editions of Macbeth place the witches meeting specifically on "The Hard Muir," the lands between Brodie and Auldearn, and the Bard's prose description of the area rings true. He also changed Calder to Cawdor for all time, by spelling it phonetically in accordance with local pronunciation.

The King's misogyny had another lasting effect on Scottish culture. He gathered together all the most extreme forms of witch paranoia and published them, in the "Daemonologie" of 1597. He thereby encouraged the persecution of thousands of women, whose fate beggars description. The notion of witchcraft was well established in Scottish culture, and practices dating from Druidic times were still found in many of the country districts. In pre- reformation days the priest could always prescribe a prayer that would take away the threat of witchcraft, and the Catholic religion had a reassuring panoply of Saints to intervene in specific cases. With Catholicism gone, the people were powerless to deal with witchcraft in non-violent ways. The Kirk took to burning witches with pious gusto, on the flimsiest of evidence. This ruthlessness fitted the new Presbyterian culture. Kirk Ministers had to reject all luxuries and earthly pleasures as sinful, and share the poverty of their parishioners. They believed public prayer to be sinful and Bible readings at funerals to be "debauchery". Celebrating Christmas or Easter was especially abhorrent, even christening celebrations were banned.

The great cathedrals and monasteries of the Catholic past were left to decay, their stained glass windows and fine carvings smashed and burned as idolatry. Newly built churches were starkly devoid of ornament or comfort. The ministers dominated their parishioners, keeping the first public records of births, marriages and deaths in Scotland, and taking responsibility for the moral health of all on their register. Some would punish violently for perceived sin. Persons adjudged to have slandered a minister could be banished from the town or cast in chains. Wives accused of nagging their husbands could be gagged with an iron bridle. Adultery and homosexual activity, common among the rich, could lead ordinary people to the stake. Above all, the Kirk feared witchcraft, and considered dancing, flirting and even cosmetics to be forms of sorcery, the pleasure of the body being a snare of Satan.

This would all have seemed perfectly normal to Alexander, the 15th Brodie of Brodie, when he became Thane in 1636, at the age of nineteen. His childhood may have been lonely, having been spent (to comply with a royal proclamation) at an English school from the age of ten. David passed away, aged 46, when Alexander was just fifteen years old. John Wyland collected him from the school, and brought him back to claim his inheritance. Alexander was lucky, in that John Wyland was there to manage the household and his uncles were there to teach him how to manage his estate. His father's brothers included the Ministers of Forres and Auldearn, and the Lairds of Lethen and Asleisk. Alexander continued his education at St. Andrews and at Aberdeen, but did not enjoy student life. He had been raised as a Presbyterian Christian, he was a quiet, gentle man, and the routine debauchery of the colleges (which maintained the culture of the previous age) depressed him. His heart was still young and light, though, for he soon found love with a beautiful young lady called Elizabeth Innes. She was the grand daughter, on her mother's side, of the Bonnie Earl of Moray. Although young, she was the widow of Urquhart of Craigstone, who had died the year before. Brodie Castle still bears their entwined monograms in the plasterwork, with lavish decoration, a striking testament to their affection in those austere times. Alexander married Elizabeth in 1635, and she bore him a daughter, Grizel, and a son, James, in the following two years. They enjoyed domestic life, embellishing their austere fortress and making it into a family home. Alexander was devoted to his beautiful and gracious wife, calling her *"The Light of his eyes"* Their decorations at Brodie show that the simplicity of their Presbyterian belief did not mean that they were miserable. They still speak to us of humour and joyful living.

Events outside their estates were gathering pace. When King James died, in 1625, the ill-fated Charles I ascended the throne. He had a "High Church" Episcopalian preference in religion. He sought to impose his views on his unwilling Scottish subjects by the imposition of a revised, compulsory, book of prayer. In 1637 the book was used in a service at St. Giles Church, in Edinburgh, resulting in a most un-Christian riot. The King ordered all those protesting against his reforms to be punished, even using the petitions of his subjects as a list of malefactors to be hunted down. Religious leaders in Edinburgh responded by drawing up a document stating the principles of their religious belief It emphasised the individual's duty to God, rejected the primacy of Kings in religious matters, and renounced Catholic forms. It ended with an oath to maintain "The True Religion" and, only secondly, "His Majesty's Authority" People queued to sign this document, the National Covenant, and copies were carried throughout the land to be signed in local Presbyteries. Those adhering to its principles became known as Covenanters, and were to define the history of Scotland for the next seventy years. The very first signature on the National Covenant was that of James Graham, the Earl of Montrose.

The Covenant was brought to Forres in April 1638, and Montrose himself visited the town to persuade the gentry to sign. Almost all did, including Alexander Brodie, his uncle Lethen, all of the Ministers except a Cumming, Hay of Lochloy and Alexander's brother in law, Kinnaird of Culbin (who was married to his sister Grizel). Nationalism played a part in the enthusiastic adoption of the Covenant. It was seen as a defence against Scotland becoming a poor province of England, by asserting the rights of the people in religious matters. The General Assembly of the Kirk of Scotland moved to abolish Episcopalian forms throughout the country, and dismissed the King's Bishops. The King was outraged, and told his Privy Council that they would have to use force to bring the Scots to heel. He began raising an army of invasion. The Magnates became aligned in this new contention. The Earl of Huntly and his Gordons were for the King. Argyll's Campbells were for the Covenant. Scots mercenaries returned from overseas in expectation of a bloody contest at home. Twenty thousand Englishmen were ordered to assemble in arms near the border. The Scots army travelled South to meet them, and after a period of stalemate, crossed into England, scattered the King's forces and captured Newcastle and Durham. The Brodie took up arms with the local militia, which was engaged to keep Huntly's Gordons in check. All that summer they marched and counter marched, fending off the Gordon threat while the army of the Covenant went from victory to victory. Then, in August 1640, Elizabeth died.

We can scarcely guess at Alexander's distress when '*the light of his eyes*' was extinguished. We hear of him spending hours walking in the woods at Brodie, as the dying summer withered the leaves and brought the cold northern winds to his home. We may imagine the anguish of his extempore prayer, as he tried to make sense of his bereavement. Brodie was destined never to marry again, and the joy of his early years was transformed by grief to a deep, tormented piety. He gave himself wholly to the cause of the Covenant, and within a few months had become a leader of its most extreme faction.

Outside of his home, the King had made peace and the Gordon threat had diminished. Yet within six months of his wife's death, Brodie led a party of fundamentalists to desecrate Elgin Cathedral, the burial place of the Gordons. They knew that Catholics were using the tumble-down remains of the *"Lantern of the North"* for secret worship. Together with Elizabeth's brother, and the Minister of Elgin, Gilbert Ross (who has been remembered as a *"detestable bigot")* Brodie destroyed two paintings, of the crucifixion and the last judgment. They went on to smash a beautiful mediaeval rosewood alter screen, which had survived the Wolf of Badenoch and the Reformation, only to perish at the hands of the "true religion". The Minister took home some of the timber as fuel for his kitchen, and was filled with superstitious horror when he found that it would not burn. The less radical Presbyterians deplored this vandalism, but the hard liners would not be challenged. For Alexander, imagery *was* idolatry.

In 1643 Alexander became Member of Parliament for Moray, and representative elder of the Forres Presbytery to the General Assembly of the Church of Scotland. In the two years since his wife's death he had become a leader of the most extreme wing of the Covenanting cause. Brodie had three determining principles. The National Religion of Scotland was to be upheld in its purity and simplicity. The King's authority was to be upheld in civil matters. The need for personal religion, the Presbyterian ethos, was to be promoted and encouraged.

 In England, the Civil war between the King and Parliament had begun. The Scottish Parliament came into the war on the parliamentary side. Their price was £30,000 a month to maintain the Scots army in the field, and Presbyterianism to be adopted as the national religion of England. When the English Parliament agreed to this "Solemn League and Covenant", a Scottish army crossed into England and gave Cromwell the victory he needed at Marston Moor. At this point, Montrose turned his coat. Perhaps he could not accept the downfall of the King. As an aristocrat himself, he must have felt the need to maintain the aristocratic principle in the face of the near - democratic Presbyterians and the levellers of the parliamentary army. In 1645 He raised an army of Highlanders and Irish mercenaries, and led a campaign against the Covenanters that was to lead to the burning of Brodie.

Montrose defeated a much larger force of Covenanters at Tippermuir, near Perth, and then advanced into Aberdeen. Here the Highlanders ran riot in a three days orgy of plunder, rape and murder. The Earl then led his men on a winter campaign through the Highlands, where many clan differences were settled in the King's name. Montrose had Lord Lewis Gordon on his staff, and many Gordon swords in his army. They fell on the Campbell stronghold of Inverary and burned it, forcing Argyll to flee for his life. Then they turned North along the Great Glen, towards Moray. On the 9th May 1645, Montrose's' army reached Auldearn. A Covenant Army was moving up to meet them, with three thousand foot and five hundred horse. The Brodie was with them, and his kin. They had all heard the stories of the sack of Aberdeen and were in no doubt of what defeat would mean at the hands of Montrose's wild army. Patrols from the two armies met in short skirmishes in the fields west of Forres during the two days preceding the battle. Montrose quartered his troops about the village of Auldearn, and climbed the tower of the old church to study the lie of the land.

Auldearn village stands on a ridge running south from the church, with a distinct hollow at the southern end, and the castle mound at the north. A few broken walls still existed at the northern end, forming enclosures where troops could be hidden from view, and there were further opportunities for concealment in the southern hollow. Montrose prominently positioned part of his force at the front of the village, but positioned two large and well- equipped reserve forces in the two hiding places. He placed a large force of highlanders, led by the Macdonalds, in the Northern enclosure, and took personal charge of eight hundred foot and fifty horse in the southern hollow. Two hundred more horsemen, with Lord George Gordon in command, were hidden behind the castle mound.

The Covenanters, under General Hurry, inadvertently gave warning of their approach. Hurry allowed his men to discharge and reload their muskets before they advanced, intending their guns to be warm and freshly charged. The crackle of musketry alerted Montrose of their approach, and gave him time to oversee their dispositions. Hurry's men moved along the line of a little brook, through a small marsh, as they approached the village. The terrain caused them to string out along the track, but they believed Montroses' army to be waiting within the village itself, and they were unaware of the ambush that had been prepared. The Macdonalds, impatient for the fray, sprang the trap prematurely. They rose suddenly from cover and rushed at the Covenanters in the wild highland charge. Hurry realised that there was still time, and swung his forces to receive the assault on the front. There was a brief, furious hail of musket fire and the two sides met with pike and sword, pushing and beating at close quarters. We may imagine Alexander struggling in the press of battle, the passion of his religion driving him to smite the foe, urging his men forward with the Covenanter battle-cry of *"Jesus and No Quarter!"* The larger Covenanter force began to push the highlanders back by sheer weight of numbers, and then the southern Royalist reserve - the unsprung half of the trap - rose from cover and took Hurry's men from the rear. Trapped between the two forces, the Covenanters could not deploy and were shot and hacked down. Hurry and his cavalry broke and fled, trampling down their own men in their haste to leave the field. Montrose sent a runner to tell the Gordon Horse to attack, with the message *"Is Macdonald to have all the honour this day?"* The two hundred horsemen rode out from cover and charged. The foot soldiers, caught in Montroses' trap, fought and died where they stood, *"...even in ranks and files, so great was the execution..."* some three thousand men died at Auldearn that day, leaving the Laigh of Moray defenceless before Montroses' murderous rabble.

In the aftermath of the battle came revenge against the Covenanter leaders. Montrose gave orders to Lewis Gordon to *"burn the place of Brodie pertaining to the Laird of Brodie "* and the highlanders fell on the undefended house, smashing, looting, and burning. Flames tore through the tower and funneled out through the windows, destroying the home, the treasures and the records of a thousand years of unbroken occupation.

Across the surrounding fields the air reeked of smoke and pinpoints of light flared in the darkness as the cottages of the Brodie estate were put to the torch. Culbin, Innes, Lethen and Burgie were also burned. Alexander of Lethen lost 800 cattle, 1800 sheep and 200 horses to the highlanders and all his estate buildings were left in flames. The village of Garmouth, at the mouth of the Spey, was burned because it belonged to the Innes family. Even the nets of the fishermen were cut, to deprive them of their livelihood. The Highlanders and Irishmen of Montrose's command distinguished themselves by their wanton cruelty and barbarism. The screams of the victims continued throughout the long and bloody night. *"Thus, as Montrose ordered, were sent out parties through the country with fire and plundering"*. Brodie's deeds of ownership of his house and lands were destroyed in the fire. In subsequent years he had to apply to parliament to have his ownership confirmed, and in his application we hear his own account of the calamity.

"We fell before the wild Irish's six times without interruption, and to mingle the Church' s and the lands calamity with my private loss, my house and my mains (home farm) and bigging (buildings) was burnt to the ground and my estate made desolate, and no place left me, nor means to subsist...your enemies are skilful to destroy. Amongst the rest in this

common calamity, the writs and evidents whereby I have title to enjoy the small estate whereto I succeeded...are wholly destroyed. I have nothing to answer if anything is claimed, though never so unjustly. "

Indeed, the night of the battle left no safe haven for Alexander or his young family, and his Innes, Dunbar and Kinnaird kin had all suffered their own calamities. Where and how they hid from the highlanders, we do not know. Six times the hostiles came through Brodie, and we can only guess at the slaughter and brutality that stained the Brodie lands. The Scottish parliament renewed Alexander's title to his estate, and granted him a limited tax exemption, to help his financial recovery. The sacking of the estate in late spring would have limited the possibilities of a good harvest, but hopefully the newly sown crops would have recovered sufficiently to provide some meal for the winter. Early in 1646, the Gordons attacked again, led by the Marquis of Huntly. This time they deliberately destroyed the means of producing crops, and left utter desolation in their wake.

Alexander and his followers were at the Inverness garrison when the attack began, but his family and tenants took shelter with his Uncle Alexander at Lethen. They gave a good account of themselves. The Gordons, with 2000 men, besieged Lethen House for twelve weeks, but their efforts at storming the building were repeatedly repulsed with heavy losses. Huntly expressed his rage by destroying the Lethen Estate, killing or driving off all but ten of the 160 occupants. He also attacked Lethen's home at Kinloss, and found the family charter chest, which was hidden beneath a hearth stone. He burned them all. As their supplies dwindled, the defenders looked constantly for assistance from Inverness or Darnaway, but none came. Secret messages were carried from the house at night, in a desperate attempt to slip past the Gordon lines, but without success. When the ammunition was all but gone, Joseph Brodie, the Minister of Auldearn, left the house under a flag of truce to negotiate with the Gordon leader.

Huntly raised the siege in exchange for a bond of £2000, made payable to him. As soon as the Gordons had gone, Brodie of Lethen re-stocked his house with food and ammunition, and raised the blue flag of the Covenant once more. The news from England, however, brought the promise of peace. King Charles had surrendered to the Scottish Army at Newark. Montrose had fled overseas, and his army had dispersed.

When Alexander returned to the Scottish parliament, he found that things were not as promising as they had appeared. The English parliament had not paid the monthly subsidies for the Scots army in the field, and the treasury was in a very poor position. Furthermore, the English Parliament was now in the grip of the Army, with Cromwell at its head, and they had no interest at all in establishing Presbyterianism in England. The Scots voted to hand over their royal prisoner to the English Parliament, in exchange for a back payment of the subsidy, but they were soon shocked to realise that Cromwell was planning to try the King for his life. If this seems ironic, it is founded on one of the basic principles of the Covenant. The Covenanters believed that the King had no right to interfere in their religious observance or to force them to accept Episcopalian forms of worship. That said, they believed in the King's right to rule them in civil, secular matters. Regicide was never part of their agenda, as it was in the English Parliament. One section of the Scottish Parliament, called "the Engagers", wanted to send an army to rescue the King. Brodie and Lethen (who was Member of Parliament for Nairn) both opposed the Engagers. Five years of warfare had turned them against the Stuart. The King was, after all, the man who had sent Huntly and Montrose to harry and destroy their homes. Too many innocents had died for the Stuart's "Divine Right", and the two Alexanders wanted it to end. The Duke of Hamilton, the leader of the Engagers, got his way, and mustered an army for the invasion of England. They burned Lethen before they left, in reprisal for Brodie's opposition. It did them little good.

The Scots met Cromwell's army at Preston, and they were cut to pieces in a three days fight. Hamilton was captured and executed. In the wake of this disaster the anti-engagers, (who were known as Whigs) led by Argyll and supported by the Brodies, seized power. They invited Cromwell to visit Scotland, and met with him in Edinburgh. Brodie argued against the King's trial, but Cromwell was adamant. Soon after he had returned to England, the news arrived that Charles had been executed. The Scots Parliament responded by declaring Charles II to be the King, which amounted to a declaration of war.

The new "King of Scots " was, at that time, living in exile at The Hague. When he heard of the death of his father, he commissioned Montrose to make war on the Scots, while simultaneously opening secret negotiations with their Parliament. When Montrose was captured, at the beginning of his new campaign, Charles made no effort to help him, and his most loyal supporter was hanged at the Market cross in Edinburgh. With his best hope of military success ended, Charles offered to support the Covenanter cause in exchange for their allegiance. Alexander Brodie of Brodie was selected as a Parliamentary Commissioner to negotiate with the King. He was tasked with persuading the Stuart to accept and personally swear the Covenant as the price of his throne. Brodie crossed the North Sea with five other Commissioners, including his friends Alexander Jaffray and the Earl of Cassilis. These three came from the sternest faction of the Covenanter movement. All had suffered at the hands of Montrose, which gave them good cause to distrust the Stuart.

Charles treated the Commission with exquisite politeness. He sent his own coach to meet them on landing, and received them in his private chamber. This did nothing to appease the Commissioners. They were Puritans, grave, patriotic, well meaning men, and they had a job to do. They were seeking a Christian King for the Throne of Scotland. They saw before them a corrupt, dissolute, oily-mannered youth who was Catholic in name, and contemptibly devoid of any moral standards in practice. They laid out their terms, uncompromising to the point of insult. The "King" was to accept the Covenant, and the authority of the Kirk. He was to abandon all treaties made with Catholic powers. He was to drive Catholics from his realm, and forbid the mass even to members of his own family. He was to establish the Presbyterian religion in England and Ireland as well as Scotland. He was to publicly beg God's forgiveness for the sin he had committed in using Montrose and his army against the Scots.

It would have been quite proper for Charles to have thrown them out, but that was never the Stuart way. Instead he lied smoothly, played for time, offered them his "word". Brodie and Jaffray wanted to break off the negotiations immediately, but the majority thought it best to keep going.

They argued that the King could be legally bound to their terms, and thereby satisfy the requirements of Parliament. Charles was in desperate straits, without an army to restore his Kingdom and without money to maintain his household in exile. The Commissioners had a draft from the Scottish Parliament for £300,000, to deal with his immediate needs. The Scots offer, though galling to his pride, would bring him power and money. He agreed to the terms, though he kept putting off actually signing the Covenant. Brodie wrote afterwards:

"I know not if our success with the King was a mercy. If his heart had been true I would have counted it so, and I did judge that we were about our duty in dealing with him...yet he discovered much disaffection, and approved his father's ways in his heart, nay, in his discourse. Now what our duty should have been, I know not; but I am apt to judge that we were hasty, inconsiderate, nay, we feared and apprehended the evil that was to come upon these lands "

Brodie drew up the documents of agreement on behalf of the Scottish Parliament. The Commissioners found that the money markets would not accept the Scottish draft, and Brodie, Cassilis and Lothian had to raise 100,000 merks on their own security to pay their "King's" expenses. They were due to sail for Scotland in the Dutch national ship *Skidam* at the beginning of June 1650. The Stuart had still not signed the Covenant. Brodie and Jaffray refused to board until he signed. *"...else we were taking along the plague of God to Scotland".* They did not realise how prophetic these words were to prove. Charles finally took the oath. The perjury in his heart was clear to at least one of the Commissioners. Alexander Jaffray wrote: *"He sinfully complied with what we sinfully pressed upon him...making him sign and swear to a covenant...that he hated in his heart. "* The ship slipped away from the Dutch coast, carrying it's unhappy cargo North, hiding from the English cruisers that could have changed world history by a chance encounter. If Charles had been brought before Cromwell, he would have met the same fate as his father. On the 23rd June 1650, the ship entered the Moray Firth, running before a storm, unaware that an English fleet was lying in wait. The same storm that brought the *Skidam* blew the English ships from their station. Watchers on the shore could see both the King's ship and the

English fleet, but they were out of sight of each other. The *Skidam* came safely to anchor in the mouth of the Spey at Garmouth. The boat that ferried the King went aground in the river, and a fisherman called Milne carried Charles to his kingdom on his back. The whole party dined with the Brodie's Father and mother-in-law at Innes House, and here Charles is said to have signed the Covenant again. The Commissioners were so distrustful of the King that they repeatedly coerced him into further concessions. He was already beginning to regret yielding to these disrespectful "subjects ".

Charles soon saw another side of his kingdom, as the people turned out to cheer him. The party travelled to Falkland Palace via the homes and Castles of the Magnates, beginning with the Catholic Huntly, who treated the King to lavish hospitality. He was the same Lewis Gordon that had burned Brodie after the Battle of Auldearn. Brodie's reaction to his hospitality is not recorded, but his grave and pious disposition would have prevented any indiscretion. In any case, Montrose was dead. Charles passed his decomposing quarters displayed on spikes at Aberdeen and Dundee, but he affected not to see them. When Alexander Brodie returned to the Scottish Parliament he received the thanks of the house for his efforts, and was made a Lord of Session (a senior justice), which made him the first Lord Brodie in history. His duty now was to serve his King and Country against the Ironside threat.

The English army under Cromwell was massing for the invasion of Scotland. The Scots, with their uncanny knack of always putting dogma before practical matters, had devised an ideological test for soldiers to pass in order to join the defence of their home. The Scots parliament preferred a weak but obedient army to one that might prefer the King to the Kirk. The dogma was that an army of true believers, however small, would be invincible. Brodie, to his credit, opposed the purges. He said, using his profound knowledge of scripture, that he knew of no word or warrant from God to bind the hands of men from their own defence. The Estates did not accept his view. They dismissed 3,000 of the most experienced men, including all the veterans of the army of the Engagers, and all the unabashed Royalists, who they described as "Malignants". So the Scots army massed before Edinburgh, putting their faith in the Lord, as well as an extensive system of trenches and fortifications. Alexander became Commissary - General, and threw himself into the work, buying supplies for the troops out of his own pocket. His Uncle, Brodie of Lethen, commanded a troop of horse. He also found large sums of money to help pay for his country's defence.

When Cromwell led his army into Scotland, he found that the southern counties had been denuded of men and supplies. They marched North through a wasted countryside, full of hungry women and children, arriving at last before Dunbar. A long stalemate ensued, with the English encamped in front of the fortified lines. During the stand-off Cromwell wrote to the General Assembly. He set out his case that a King, taken in by the Scots, should not be imposed on the English, especially as that King was the very head of the Royalist Catholics. Cromwell's tone was passionate: *"I beseech you, in the bowels of Christ, think it possible you may be mistaken"*. Alexander must have read Cromwell's plea when it was brought to the Assembly. Knowing the King, and knowing that the Englishmen before Edinburgh were fervent co-religionists to the Scots, he may very well have thought it possible that he was mistaken. But no one wants their mistakes to be pointed out to them by an invading army.

The defensive positions prepared by the Scots almost won the war for them. Incessant rain and shortages of supplies, squalid conditions and heavy losses by disease, lowered the invader's morale. But their Commanding Officer was Oliver Cromwell, and when they attacked they did so to a beautifully planned and orchestrated design, which rolled up the Scots defences like a carpet and pushed them back three quarters of a mile in the first assault. Both sides sang psalms and hymns as they went into battle, and both sides believed that they were doing the Lord's work. The Lord favoured Cromwell that day, and his work left three thousand good men dead on the field, and ten thousand more as prisoners. Alexander Jaffray was among the prisoners, and he had been wounded four times during the action. His wounds probably saved his life. Cromwell released the five thousand wounded prisoners the day after the battle. Those still fit to fight were sent to England, where they were kept in appalling conditions. Most died. About 1,000 were used, as slave labour, to drain the marshes of East Anglia, another 1000 were sent as slaves to the Americas. Few were to see their homes again.

Cromwell's forces now occupied Edinburgh, and the Scots had to raise a new army to expel him. The Kirk party were being forced to accept that ideological purity was now a secondary consideration to military capacity. There was an ugly rumour that the King had fallen to his knees and given thanks to God when he had heard of the Scots defeat. It was also believed that the King had been conspiring with the Catholic Magnates, especially Lord Lewis Gordon, the Marquis of Huntly. The fact that the King was preparing a coup was not known, but the fact that he was in contact with the powerful dissidents was. Alexander Brodie and Johnstone of Wariston were selected to purge the King's Guards.

The King sent word to Atholl and Huntly, warning them of the forthcoming purge. A plan was hastily concocted. Atholl's Highlanders would infiltrate Perth. The guards would arrest Brodie and Wariston, and then signal the highlanders, who would seize control of the town. A second force of highlanders would seize Dundee. An army of Gordons under Huntly would rendezvous with the King. Charles would be left in control of all Scotland North of Perth. It could have worked, but it required a quality of courage that Charles did not possess. He went into Perth on the night of the coup, decided that there were not enough Highlanders present to carry the plot through, and ran away. Those loyal highlanders that did rise found themselves unsupported. The attempt quickly collapsed. Charles was found the next day hiding in a hovel, having fled for forty miles but ending up lost and exhausted. Huntly and Atholl, and all their brave followers were perplexed. They did not know that Charles had another plan of his own. He had intended to use the rising as a cover, flee to Holland and leave his supporters to face the consequences alone.

Even so, Charles' coronation at Scone was to go ahead. Alexander attended in his capacity as a Lord of Session. The ceremony was a curious affair in which the High Church elements of the ancient ritual had been purged, and replaced with Presbyterian correctness. The Duke of Argyll placed the Crown of Scotland on the Stuart's head. Charles took the Covenant once again during the ceremony, affirming before God and his subjects that:

"I, Charles,...do assure and declare, by my solemn oath, in the presence of Almighty God, the searcher of hearts, my allowance and approbation of the National Covenant and the Solemn League and Covenant, and fully establishing Presbyterial Government...that I shall observe these in my own practice and family, and shall never make opposition to these, or endeavour any change thereof."

It is doubtful whether Alexander believed him on that occasion, either. The King presented The Brodie with a Van Dyke portrait of Charles I, which still hangs today in the drawing room of Brodie Castle. This graven image must have been galling for Lord Brodie to receive. He had far more in common with Cromwell's puritans than he did with the Stuarts, Covenanted or not. The new Scots army did not succeed in driving Cromwell out. In a bold and desperate gamble, the Scots leaders turned their men South to invade England. They believed that the English would flock to their standard, to support the King and the True Religion. Perhaps they might have, had the King and true religion not come to them in arms at the head of a foreign army. For the English, this was a straightforward case of foreign invasion, and the banner they flocked to was Cromwell's.

The Scots army fortified the ancient city of Worcester, broke the bridges over the Severn, and prepared for a long siege. It did not come. On the 3rd September 1651, one year to the day after the Battle of Dunbar, Cromwell's troops crossed the River on bridges made of boats lashed together, and stormed the town. Within two hours, the King was a fugitive, 2,000 Scots were dead in the streets, and a further ten thousand taken as prisoners. A number of Brodie kinsmen and tenants were among those captured at Worcester. One died in prison in London, a few returned to Dyke. They had to swear an affidavit about the death of their comrade, so that his wife could legally remarry. Most disappeared into the slave labour system, in the marshes of the fens or the plantations of America. One in ten of the young men of Scotland had fallen in the wars. The country was bankrupt, famished, exhausted. General Monck captured the Scottish Parliament, and dispersed it. Scotland was now an English province. Brodie, dismissed from office, was told to go home. But he was not to be left in peace.

Cromwell consolidated his hold on Scotland by the systematic deployment of military bases. He caused a chain of forts to be built, securing the main routes through the highlands. He placed garrisons in the towns, and taxed the people to pay for them. He intended to make the forced Union of the two nations permanent, and for that purpose he invited Alexander Brodie to take office under his provisional Government. There was nothing opportunist about Alexander. He had to weigh the possibilities of service to the Lord in serving or rejecting the Lord Protector, and no earthly considerations of power, wealth or patriotism could dictate to his conscience. He writes:

"Oh Lord, I have met with the Lion and the Bear before, but this is the Goliath. The strongest and the greatest temptation is the last. "

Days of contemplation, prayer and reflection followed. Alexander had the gift of seeing himself in the third person, and that often shows in his writing. We cannot doubt that he was too hard on himself, but then, who are we to judge a man who felt that his every action was to be weighed in the sight of God? Alexander drew his conclusions:

"He would surely be blasted and corrupt and wither, if he lost communion with the Lord and followed great employments. "

So the answer was No. Alexander's common sense gave him another maxim in support of his judgment: No usurpation ever lasts long. Alexander arrived home in mid June 1653. Six weeks later a large patrol of Cromwell's Ironsides arrived at Brodie. They were going North to search for the Earl of Glencairn, who was leading a highland force in a guerrilla war against the occupation. The leader of the troop. Captain Deal, quartered his men in Brodie's "Little Park" a grove of young oak and birch trees that he had planted with Elizabeth in happier times. The little plantation was wrecked. Alexander was forced, by inexorable Presbyterian logic, to conclude that the Lord was punishing him for loving his trees too much. A few days later another troop came through, on their way to reinforce Deal. Glencairn's Highlanders had been located in the hills near Inverness. The Highlanders, in their own country, were unbeatable. But the Ironside forts and patrols were hemming them in to the inhospitable mountains and cutting off their supplies. To Cromwell, and perhaps to Brodie, Glencairn's Jacobites were little more than bandits. Certainly Glencairn saw Brodie as a target, and in January 1654, he tried to attack him. Brodie received a letter from Glencairn on The 10th January, demanding his surrender. A second letter followed soon after, this time demanding money. Alexander embarked on a long communion with his maker, seeking advice on whether to flee or pay the blackmail. In the end he chose to do neither, but to wait patiently and trust in God. Within a few days, heavy rain caused the Findhom to rise and flood, cutting off the fords in the lower valleys. At the same time, troopers hunting for Glencairn arrived at Darnaway. Brodie gave thanks for special providence, unaware that Glencairn, driven higher up the river, had attacked his family at Lethen, burned down the house and sacked the granaries, and left the poor folk destitute in the midst of a highland winter.

Brodie rebuked himself for misunderstanding God's intentions, thanked him for the safety of the survivors, and set to work relieving the poor with oats and grain from his own stock. There was nothing theoretical about Alexander's Christianity. He was known as *"The Good Laird of Brodie"* in his own lifetime, and remembered as a cheerful and generous soul. His inner torments were not allowed to intrude on his neighbours. Lethen was one of the finest houses in Moray, but there is no mourning for its destruction in the Brodie diaries. The Brodie and twenty members of his family, representing all the branches of the name, gathered together in the burned out ruins. There, amidst the blackened stonework and the sodden, charred timbers, they renewed their Covenant with God.

Alexander's chosen path meant that there were no quick fixes for his future, or his nation. The Jacobites holding out for the Stuart cause were, on the whole, the same Highland bandits that had plagued the Laigh for centuries, whatever their ostensible cause. The English Garrisons were the most effective Police force the Laigh had ever known. The English men were, on the whole, a decent set, whose Puritan religion had much in common with the Presbyterian Scots. Their presence brought high taxes, but it also brought stability after war and benefits to both agriculture and trade. It is said that English soldiers first brought Kale to Scotland, and the knitting of woolen stockings. Some of the soldiers married and settled locally, bringing new agricultural techniques to the Laigh. The Presbyteries found difficulty in dealing with the occupation. As a Usurpation it had to be wicked, but they could hardly want the Stuart back. They could not speak of Parliament, as their lawful parliament had been dismissed. Cromwell was a tyrant and a Regicide, even if his works seemed good. It was deeply puzzling for the true religion. They took to calling the Government "The Present Power", and in time they almost approved of it. Grain ripened in the fields, and was not trampled. The swords of the Magnates stayed in their sheaths.

Alexander's daughter Grizel, now aged 18, married Dunbar of Grangehill, and James went to study at Aberdeen University. Lethen sold the stone from the old Abbey lands at Kinloss to the English, and it was built into the Cromwellian fort at Inverness. The Brodie sold some of the oaks from his forests, and sent shiploads of grain abroad. All were enjoying the blessings of peace. The Brodie was always prepared to express his views to the Ironside Officers that visited his home, and occasionally they would pray together. By contrast, he had been arguing with Murdoch Mackenzie, the Minister of Elgin, who combined bigotry with aggression in equal measure. Mackenzie believed ordinary people incapable of leading extempore prayer or interpreting the gospel. He believed in his duty to interpret their religion for them, a deviation from Presbyterianism that Brodie was quick to point out, but unable to persuade. Alexander believed passionately in Religious Instruction within the family and the power of prayer within the home. Mackenzie had once been a Chaplain in the Swedish Army, and had blessed a hundred grim slaughters before the Scottish troubles had brought him home. He made it his business, every Sunday, to visit those not at the Kirk and upbraid them. He would tour the Parish every Christmas day, to ensure that no one was celebrating. A joyless man.

On the other hand, Colonels Witham and Scroop of the Army of the Protectorate were willing to discuss the Westminster confession of faith, or the true interpretation of scripture, with the lively pleasure of the true believer, and The Brodie enjoyed their visits. One day Alexander asked them how they could prove that the occupation was truly for the good of the people. They replied that *"it would help the people most if honest men would accept employment"* a home thrust on Brodie's refusal to serve "The Present Power" in any capacity. The King's exile seemed permanent, and no true believer could want him back in charge of the country. The present power sought justice and toleration. The Puritans ruling Britain were as fervent in the Lord as The Brodie could wish. Even Johnstone of Wariston, one of the authors of the Covenant, had become a member of the Westminster Parliament. Alexander returned to his bench as a Lord of Session, and later accepted employment under Cromwell as a Justice of the peace.

Alexander had been sitting in judgment on his own lands since he had taken possession of them, at the age of 19. He was known to be a fair and serious minded man who would listen carefully to his people. He would admonish, commend or reprove his tenants as he saw the need, but rarely evicted or punished. He gave rent rebates to the industrious as their due, and to the feckless as charity. The "Good Laird of Brodie" would be an ornament to the present power's judiciary.

In September 1658, Cromwell died, and his son became Lord Protector. It appeared that the "Present Power" was to become hereditary. The following summer, John Wyland died. He had witnessed all the feuds and battles, and all the joys and triumphs, of three generations at Brodie. Alexander wrote:

"Scarce are there any living now in these bounds which had been here in my father's or Grandfathers time, which was but yesterday. Oh, so soon does one generation pass, and another come, so do our days glide away like the stream or like the shadow"

That same summer Alexander's son James married the beautiful Lady Mary Kerr, the daughter of the Earl of Lothian, who had been on the commission to the King with Brodie. James was to become the 16th Brodie of Brodie, and his marriage happy, fruitful and long.

Outside of the estate, dark clouds were gathering again. Richard Cromwell failed as the leader of "Great Britain" Within a year, the second Charles Stuart was on the Throne, as vindictive and treacherous as his forebears, with a long list of scores to settle. He broke his oaths to the Covenant with a sneer that *"Presbyterianism...is not a religion for gentlemen"*

Suddenly, all the hard won religious freedoms were at risk again. The obnoxious prayer book was reintroduced. Episcopacy, the rule of Bishops, was imposed. Glencairn became Chancellor of Scotland. Argyll, who had placed the Crown of Scotland on Charles' head, was summarily beheaded. James Guthrie and Johnstone of Wariston were hanged. A committee of fining was set up by the King to pursue his lesser opponents, and Alexander was on their list. He was dismissed from his office of Lord of Session. It was possible that his entire estate would be forfeited. His only hope lay in travelling to London to plead his case, and that was what he did. In July 1661, in company with the Laird of Cawdor, he began the long ride south. The relative wealth of England and the rich fertility of its agriculture impressed The Brodie. He admired, with a farmer's eye, the rich grasslands around Durham, although he could not bring himself to admire the Bishop of Durham's palace. He saw the noble parks and vineyards of Hatfield House, and came at last to London:

"I saw a mighty City, numerous, many souls in it, great plenty of all things, and thought him a great King that had so many at command. "

He visited the Old St. Paul's Cathedral, and the Royal Exchange. He explored London's book shops, buying several works of Greek and Roman history, Geography, a large atlas, a life of Sir Walter Raleigh and a large quarto Bible. He thought of them as light reading. He sat in on the Services at Westminster Abbey, but could take no pleasure in religious music and the ancient pieties. He found himself much more at home in the Presbyterian Kirk in Foster Lane. He bought dinner for his former colleague, Sharp, a leading Covenanter who had turned his coat and had been rewarded by being made Archbishop of St. Andrews. Sharp was a devious political animal, much given to lying and treachery. He used the Brodie ruthlessly, and did him harm, under pretence of friendship. Sharp denounced Brodie as a dissenter, and would not acknowledge him in public, although he claimed in private to be "helping" him. Glencairn, the burner of Lethen and a deadly enemy to the Brodie, led the Scots faction at Court. After three futile months in

London, Alexander knew that he was wasting his time:

"My desire is to The Lord to rid me of this place. It is a place I have no fellowship in...I am doing no good in it...I desire to be restored to those I am tied to, for The Lords glory."

On the 14th May 1662, Alexander kissed the King's hand and left for the eight-day journey home. He remembered his time in London as *"Exiled, discountenanced, maligned, hated, persecuted, opposed, friendless, witless, great ones against me!"* There is a dark lantern on display today in Brodie, said to have been the very one carried by Guy Fawkes during his attempt to blow up James Stuart in 1605. Alexander may have bought it as a souvenir of London. We may imagine his relief when he eventually saw the gaunt tower among the trees, and knew that he was home. His trials were not yet over. The Committee of Fining still had to decide on his punishment for being disliked by the King... and back at home, there had been *"A great discovering "* of Witchcraft.

The "Discovering" had begun while the Brodie was in London, and had started with the arrest of Isobel Gowdie of Auldearn. The Reverend Harry Forbes, a local minister, claimed that she had used magic to tip him out of bed at night. Isobel said that she could turn herself into a cat or a jackdaw, and gave her enthralled interrogators a wealth of detail about satanic pacts and curses, baptisms of blood, all the trash of common belief in witchcraft.

She said that she had first met the devil in the tower of Auldearn Church in 1647. At that time, soon after Montrose had been through, the town was still in ruins, half the agricultural land was waste, three thousand corpses were new buried around the village and not enough living men were left to till the fields. Isobel may have suffered personally at the invaders hands. The Devil had certainly been in Auldearn, and his works were all around.

Isobel's "Confessions" indicted twelve other women and three men. All were found guilty. Accusations also fell on Katherine Sowter, Janet Breidhead and Janet Bandon. They gave a dozen more names under interrogation, and the circle of fire began to spread. Among the accused were two women of Forres, Isobel Simson and Isobel Elder.

Brodie took expert advice. He consulted with John Colville, a Member of the General Assembly who had studied with Matthew Hopkins, the notorious "Witch finder General" of England. They met together at Brodie to plan their campaign. Neither of these two intelligent, well-meaning men had any doubt about what they were doing. For educated men in the seventeenth century, witchcraft was as real a menace as greenhouse gases and ozone depletion today. They could not see the devil, but they were aware of his attacks on their society through his servants, the witches. They could see the murrain that was spreading among the cattle. They had to identify and destroy Satan's recruits by the most effective means available. Witches could be "pricked" with a large bradawl to identify patches without feeling, the marks of the devil. Long periods without sleep helped witches to confess. Straightforward flogging sometimes did the job. It was unpleasant work, Alexander called it *"a work of darkness,"* but he was never one to shirk his duty. The "Good Laird of Brodie," a model of Christian compassion, agonised over the proceedings in his private diary, but remained remorseless in public. Eventually, Judgment was reached:

"... The poor creatures were found guilty, and condemned to die. The witnesses agreed clearly and fully, but Satan hardened them to deny...Grange was not clear... he was averse to the sentence of death. "

Nevertheless, the sentence stood. Arrangements had to be made to strangle and burn the women at the stake.

"They did recommend it to the Bailey of Forres to take care of the prisoners and provide for their execution...! desired not to be looked on as the pursuer of these poor creatures, and therefore left it on them. "

No doubt he slept better for doing so. The Bailey had to purchase the wooden stakes, rope, tar and peat, and set the stage for the edifying public spectacle. The stakes were set up near the town gallows, on the right hand side of the road to Elgin (now Victoria Road). Three days after their "trial", the two Isobels perished in the fire of righteousness, proclaiming their innocence until the strangling rope choked off their voices.

"In the afternoon, Isobel Elder and Isabel Simson were burnt at Forres: died obstinate; and the Lord seems to shut the door, so that wickedness should not be discovered nor expelled out of the land... "

While Alexander struggled with Satan's forces in the form of the two hapless women, the King continued to attack the Presbyterian Constitution of Scotland. Twelve local Ministers were removed from office, and replaced with Episcopalian placemen. Murdoch Mackenzie, a bigot with whom Brodie had often clashed, was made Bishop of Moray. Anxiety beset Brodie, even in his sleep. He dreamed that he was in his own home, trying to take out the Atlas that he had bought in London. Mackenzie appeared, and prevented him. Alexander felt that the dream meant that he would not be allowed to live quietly at home.

The news from London confirmed this, the Committee of Fining was discussing penalties for Brodie as high as £40,000, which would both destroy the Estate and put Alexander into a debtor's prison. Friends urged him to settle the estate on his son, while there was time. Alexander hesitated. Although James was to prove steadfast in the cause of the Covenant he showed, at that time, the symptoms of youthful folly. His father did not trust him with the Estate.

When the penalty was announced, it may have come as a relief. The fine was to be £4,800 and Brodie declared to be "Incapable of any Public Trust." This last slander was to prove heaven-sent, as it precluded the Brodie from having to take the Test Oath, the penalty for which failure would have been confiscation of the estate and banishment to the plantations. Lethen was fined £8000 and Cawdor £12,000. And this was only the beginning of the persecution.

The dismissal of the Presbyterian Ministers did not cause the people to abandon their religion. Open-air services, called "Conventicles" were organised. One banished Minister, James Urquhart, held Conventicles at Penick, between Auldearn and Insoch. People would walk for miles to attend the gatherings, and hear the forbidden sermons. The King responded with a law that made preaching at a Conventicle punishable by death. It became illegal for more than four people to meet together for prayer, except in an "established" Church. Any person failing to attend the approved Church for more than three Sundays in a row would be subject to a severe fine. Accepting the ministrations of an "outed" Minister would be punished by fines or banishment. Fortunately for the Covenanters, the hereditary Sheriff of Nairnshire was Sir Hugh Campbell of Cawdor, Brodie's nephew by his sister Elizabeth, and he approved of the Presbyterian resistance. He would collect the fines, and then quietly return them. He repeatedly risked his own life and estates to help the cause. When an imprisoned "Field Preacher" was given into Sir Hughes custody for transportation to Edinburgh for trial, he made him Chaplain to his household.

After six months, Cawdor accompanied the preacher to Edinburgh, and stood by him in the court. Whether it was by the moral pressure of Sir Hughes presence, or the thousands of Campbell swords that he represented, the result was an acquittal. The Brodie had no such armed might to reinforce his conscience. One spring day, as he walked to Dyke Church for a service of thanksgiving for the King, he stopped, turned, and went home. For almost ten years, Alexander was to maintain passive and active resistance to the Stuart. He refused the help of Falconer, the Minister of Dyke, even when James fell dangerously ill. He defied the laws on Church attendance, spending his "Solitary Sabbaths" in prayer and meditation. He sheltered refugees from persecution and appointed a field preacher, Alexander Dunbar, as his private Chaplain.

He survived an attempt by the Earl of Moray to have him charged with holding Conventicles. Brodie, Lethen, Calder and Kilravock together subscribed to a secret fund to support outed ministers. During this period it becomes clear that Alexander was re-evaluating his beliefs. During a discussion with his old friend Alexander Jaffray, he agreed that the Covenant was the work of man, and thereby fallible. Alexander Dunbar, (who had recorded the confession of Isobel Gowdie), no longer believed in the existence of witchcraft, which must have given Alexander food for thought. And the Brodie had come to realise that the continental Protestants were as steadfast and faithful as their Scots counterparts. He identified the "material parts" of religion, and became less dogmatic in the manner of its observance. But he would not attend the Episcopalian services, or accept the persecution.

Life on the estate went on regardless of the Government. Cattle and crops had to be raised, peat cut for fuel, rent courts held. Alexander took his responsibilities very seriously, visiting sick tenants, supplying schoolbooks to the children of the estate, and supporting the efforts of his people. He noted that the more industrious tenants on poor holdings enjoyed more prosperity than the less industrious on better land, but he was fair and even-handed to both.

Secret Conventicles continued to be held throughout the country. Troops were sent to break them up, but the Covenanters believed they would be rewarded by heaven for martyrdom, so the fights were often bloody and long. The Western Covenanters, that had led the coup of 1649, were ready to rebel. Then Archbishop Sharp met a band of them on the road. They dragged him from his coach and butchered him. Soon after Sharp's murder three troops of Government dragoons (under Graham of Claverhouse, of whom more later) were routed by a Covenanter mob. The King ordered a force to be raised to carry out reprisals, and put it under the command of the Duke of Monmouth, who was, in every sense, the King's foremost bastard. Brodie was shocked by the murder of his old adversary:

"It grieves my soul to hear that any professing real grace should fall in such an act...it (the murder) will do more harm to religion than his life had done or could have done. "

The King ordered the gentry of Moray to raise their followers to join Monmouth's army. The Brodie was at a loss what to do, he did not want to invite reprisals by refusing the order, but he could not take arms against his fellow Covenanters. In the end, his horses were taken from him by force, and he sent his quota of men, although he would not lead them or allow James to go in his place. It was an ugly, messy compromise that satisfied no one. Elizabeth Brodie, the daughter of John Brodie of Pluscarden was dismayed by the events.

"My relations that should have been there...with those that have taken

their lives in their hands, even they were strengthening the enemy... by sending out others."

She was destined to marry a man who had taken part in the rebellion.

Sending his followers did not absolve the Brodie or his kin from joining the King's host. Fate lent a hand. For the first time in a generation the Fiery cross was carried through the Laigh. The Macdonalds were attacking! The Gentry of the neighbourhood stood to with their followers in what proved to be a false alarm. The Brodie tried to use the defensive muster to pardon his failure to join the King's host, but to no avail. Once again the tyrannical Stuart threatened him with punishment. Monmouth's forces shattered the Covenanters at the Battle of Bothwell Brig, and the persecution grew to a new intensity. Brodie's health cracked under the strain. In one of his last diary entries he wrote longingly of his desire for a cottage in the wilderness. On his deathbed the Good Laird of Brodie told his family that "The Lord will redeem his people"... alas that he did not see the day. On the fifth of May 1680, Alexander was laid in the family vault at Dyke Church. William Falconer, the King's approved Minister conducted the Service. James was now the 16th Brodie of Brodie.

James was a very different character from his father. A bluff, hearty man, he was staunch for the Covenant but given to hard drinking and worldly pursuits. He was much harder on his tenants than his father. He quickly resorted to an armed muster of his followers in a dispute with Culbin over the peat moss at Bankhead. He was suspected of disaffection (rightly, by Stuart standards), and he received a heavy fine for his non-attendance at the King's host. The persecution of the Covenanters was reaching new depths of violence. It was the beginning of the period still remembered as "The Killing Times". The King ordered torture and summary execution to be used to persuade the population to abandon their Kirk. His instrument of choice, for persuasion, was an iron boot into which wedges were driven. A gravestone in Ayr still reads: *"Boots, thumbkins, gibbets were in fashion then: Lord, let us never see such days again."*

The dragoons enforcing the persecution were under orders *to "...turn out all the wives and children...from their habitations, if it shall appear they have conversed with their parents or husbands. "* The Stuart had publicly sworn the Covenant Oath, but he drove children out to die because their parents had done the same. Prominent among the persecutors was John Graham of Claverhouse, known to Jacobite apologists as "Bonny Dundee" but to his contemporaries as "Bloody Clavers" His style was to ask the victim, once, if they would take the Test Oath, which acknowledged the King's superiority in all causes, including religion. If they would not take the test, they were killed on the spot. There is an account of him asking a woman, as she collected up the brains of her dead husband, what she thought of him now? She replied *"I thought ever much good of him, and more now than ever "* Clavers then told her *"It were but justice to lay thee beside him... "* There is a memorial to her husband, Andrew Brodie, in the Kirk at Forgundenny. Clavers "Justice" brought destruction and misery to thousands whose only crime was Christian belief. The pressures on the Covenanters to accept Martyrdom should not be under estimated. It was a central tenet of their faith that God would try them, and that they would have to endure. One local man, Alexander Davidson, renounced the Covenant when imprisoned by the Earl of Moray. He was released only to go mad with grief at his own betrayal.

James, perhaps chastened by the fine, attended the Kirk, but his wife, Mary Kerr, would not. Alexander Dunbar was still family chaplain to the Brodie's, but his presence only increased official suspicions. The law made heritors responsible for their wife's behaviour and the time was fast approaching when James would be arrested for Mary's refusal to attend Kirk. He was facing ruin, but he would not seek to influence Mary in such a matter of conscience. Eventually, family needs overcame Mary's will to resist, and she stood by her husband in the Kirk. We may imagine the Reverend Falconer's satisfaction at seeing such a prominent dissident brought to heel. The Episcopalian Clergy were the principal informers for non-attendance, and Sir Hugh Campbell's restraint in enforcing the law had been noted by the authorities. A commission was appointed to try those in the area suspected of nonconformity. James rode to Elgin to meet them, and saw the gallows that they had caused to be erected in the town. He noted that they looked "Stern and Squint" at him. He dined with them that day, and received their summons the next. He and Mary were to be tried for holding Conventicles (a capital offence) and absence from the Kirk.

When James and Mary returned to Elgin for the trial, they found the town to be crowded with other accused persons, and many of their kin among them. Brodie of Lethen was to be tried, as was his sister Janet (who was married to George Pringle, a leading Covenanter) and his son-in-law, the Laird of Grant. Francis Brodie of Milton, Francis Brodie of Windyhills, James Brodie of Kinloss and David Brodie of Pitagavenie were also among the accused, as were Mrs Campbell of Torrich, Park of Insoch, James Urquhart, (who had often led prayers at Brodie during the 15th Thane's "Solitary Sabbaths"), and George Meldrum. The Brodie's conscience was troubled by the trial. He knew that he could be hanged or sent into slavery by the commission. They could impose fines that would ruin the estate. Even so, he felt that to lie to them would be to deny his convictions. James did attend Conventicles. To be part of a large, orderly gathering for communal worship was a crime in Stuart Britain, but it hardly sinned against the laws of God. The Commission required all of the accused to take a bond that they would obey the Stuart law. Refusal would obviously influence the Commissioners:

"There was a bond subscribed which I cannot justify my taking...a bond to live orderly, to apprehend vagrant ministers, not to suffer them to live on our ground, and many such things as these are... "

James would not comply.

James and Mary were tried separately. Both defended themselves by saying that they had prayed and read the scriptures with their private chaplain, Alexander Dunbar. Their neighbours and kinfolk, the Kinnairds of Culbin, were among the witnesses against them. James denied attending Conventicles.

"I was called to answer to my libel. I disowned frequenting Conventicles without my own house. This is to decline fines and punishment. Is there any guilt in this before God...Oh! What is become of all my resolutions?"

James and Mary were fined £25,000 Scots (£2,000 Sterling) for keeping an unlicensed Chaplain. Alexander Dunbar was sentenced to banishment to the plantations, a virtual sentence of slavery. In the interim he was to be imprisoned on the Bass Rock. Brodie of Lethen was fined £40,500 Scots. The Laird of Grant received a similar fine, Francis Brodie of Milton £10,000. David Brodie of Pitagavenie was fined and sentenced to imprisonment in Blackness Castle, as were George Meldrum and James Urquhart. Mrs. Campbell of Torrich could have walked free if she had undertaken to attend the Episcopalian Church. She refused, and was sent into slavery. The Commission had filled all the prison space in Elgin, but they were still sentencing when news came from the South. Charles II was dead. The new King of Britain was James VII, the former Duke of York, known in Scotland as the Duke of Albany, or more succinctly, *"That Beast"*

After the torture and oppression of Charles II's reign, we might hope that any successor would be an improvement. Alas for his subjects, James VII was a Stuart King, as stupid, wicked and tyrannical as his predecessors. He refused to take the Coronation Oath for Scotland. The Oath would have bound him to uphold the Protestant Reformed Religion, and this would have interfered with his plans to re-establish Roman Catholicism. He settled on a plan to deal with religious conflict in the North. Mass murder. Giving or taking the Covenant Oath, preaching at or attending a Conventicle, became punishable by summary execution without trial. Every soldier became judge and executioner. "Bloody Clavers" was back in his element, riding with his dragoons across the moors, hunting Christians for their sport. Women were staked out on beaches for the tide to drown them, mothers and daughters together, singing hymns as they waited for the tide. The first twelve months of the new reign were remembered as the "Black Year"

James tried in vain to have his fine reduced. He asked that the money his father had paid to defray Charles II's expenses be taken into account, again without success. James saw the kangaroo court's decision as the will of God:

"One of the days I was fined £2000 sterling. The world has been my idol, and the love of it, and covetousness, the root of much evil, and the Lord may justly punish me in this. "

During this period an outlawed Covenanter refugee named James Nimmo arrived in the area. He was a farmer's son from Linlithgow, who had joined the rebellion of the Western Covenanters and fought against Monmouth at Bothwell Brig. He was trying to reach the coast, to flee to Holland. During his escape he met the Laird of Park, who employed him as his factor, under an assumed name. Nimmo became a familiar figure at the Conventicles, and at these forbidden services he met Elizabeth Brodie, the beautiful daughter of John Brodie of Pluscarden. Park was struggling under a mass of fines, which were in time to beggar the estate and leave Insoch a ruin. The frequent visits of bailiffs and Sheriff's men made Park too dangerous for Nimmo, and Brodie of Lethen took him in.

Elizabeth Brodie and James Nimmo kept up a discreet correspondence, and were married in secret. Tom Hogg, a Field Preacher and an old friend of the 15th Thane, conducted the Presbyterian service. A spurned suitor. Lord Doune, stumbled across Nimmo's secret and denounced him to the authorities.

As the dragoons rode up to the house at Pluscarden, Nimmo fled to the ruins of the ancient Abbey. He found a dark comer in a monk's cell, and concealed himself there. He lay silent as the dragoons searched the ruins, noisily crashing around in the darkness... but the dragoons were highly experienced in this type of search. After they had apparently moved on, Nimmo crept from his hiding place and walked right into them, waiting silently in the darkness. They tried to seize him, but Nimmo slipped from their grasp and ran for his life. He reached Lethen ahead of the hunters, and met Elizabeth. Alexander gave them horses, and they rode clear in the dark, eventually reaching safety in Holland. The troopers interrogated John Brodie of Pluscarden. During the search they found the marriage certificate, but were confounded to discover that the names on it had been left blank.

The affair brought reprisals. Troopers scoured the area, and the Test was applied mercilessly. Unknown to all, as old Alexander Brodie had prophesied on his deathbed, the Lord was about to redeem his people. The English Parliament, sickened by the tyranny of the Stuart, invited Mary, the Protestant daughter of the King, and her husband William of Orange to take the throne. King James abandoned his kingdom and fled to the continent. With an abruptness that must have stunned the Presbyterians, the "Killing Times" were over. William Falconer, the Episcopalian minister of Dyke, fled the county and was replaced by a Western Covenanter, the Reverend Alexander Forbes. Alexander Dunbar, Thomas Hogg and David Brodie returned from prison. Alexander became Minister of Auldearn, David a Kirk Elder. David subsequently inherited the Lethen Estate, which had narrowly escaped destruction by the punitive fines. Thomas Hogg was offered the position of private chaplain to King William, but declined it. James Nimmo and Elizabeth returned from Holland, and James went on to become the City treasurer of Edinburgh.

During 1689 a Convention of the Estates was held to decide on the succession to the Throne of Scotland. William and Mary put forward a moderate agenda, but James, writing from exile in France, was threatening and bitter. He told the Scots to return to their duty or face the consequences. His supporters, led by John Graham of Claverhouse (Viscount Dundee, Bonny Dundee, Bloody Clavers) then walked out. The Convention chose William and Mary. The Presbyterian Constitution of Scotland was restored. For the Brodies of Morayshire, or for most of them, this decision was the vindication of all they stood for. "Bloody Clavers" had left to raise an army in the highlands, and the Gordons under Huntly had seized Edinburgh Castle, but the armed forces of Great Britain were with the Kirk.

Claverhouse won the backing of the Macdonalds and Macleans, who sent out the fiery cross to summon their followers to war. In a foretaste of the 18th Century, the great issues of the Royal Succession were not explained to the "Jacobite Clans". They either obeyed the summons or their homes were burned. They met the forces of Government in a furious downhill charge at the Pass of Killiecrankie, and routed them. It is said that the redcoats behind saw the great spray of blood as the Clansmen's swords bit into the front rank, and they broke, and fled, and were hunted down and butchered by the whooping Highlanders. There was a belief, among the Covenanters, that Claverhouse was an incarnation of Satan himself. He was once seen, in attacking a Conventicle, to ride his horse across the sheer cliff above the Grey Mares

Tail waterfall, where a mountain goat might have fallen to it's death. It was well known that no mortal weapon could kill him, and he may have believed it himself. Certainly one wounded redcoat on the field of Killiecrankie believed it. He drew the charge of his musket, and replaced the lead musket ball with a silver button from his own coat. He shot "Bloody Clavers" at close range, and the button tore a hole through his steel breastplate and buried itself in his black heart. When King Billy was told of the defeat at Killiecrankie, he declined advice to reinforce his armies in Scotland. *"There is no need"* he said, *"Claverhouse is dead"* And he was right.

James and Mary's later life was not entirely calm. There was a land dispute with the Kinnairds of Culbin, no doubt embittered by the memory of their testimony at the Elgin trials. When court actions failed, both sides took to mustering their followers in arms, and scenes reminiscent of the 13th Thanes day were enacted once more at Brodie. The weather at the end of the 17th Century took a consistent turn for the worse, and once more, famine stalked the land. People came to call these days *"King William's Hard Years,"* and the Jacobites - supporters of the exiled Stuart - called them a Judgment of God. Locally, there occurred one of the strangest weather disasters ever to befall Scotland.

Looking West from Findhorn village across Findhorn bay we see today the edge of the great Culbin Forest, which grows from a desert of gigantic sand dunes, once called "The Scottish Sahara". The dunes cover Culbin, once one of the most fertile estates in Scotland. Generations of the Kinnaird family raised wheat and black cattle on its rich soil. Local history is full of natural calamities, but none more dramatic than that which destroyed the Culbin Estate. The Manor house of Kinnaird of Culbin (who was married to Alexander's sister Grizel) dominated the estate. There were also sixteen farms, numerous small cottages, a few scattered crofts and the little fishing village by the Findhorn. When the sandstorm struck in October 1694, just one farm survived. There are tales of a cloud of sand two miles broad, blotting out the sun; of a river of sand spilling like water across the fields, of men releasing horses from their ploughs and wading through sand already calf deep, fighting to reach safety through the stinging, blinding air. Some inhabitants woke to find their windows blacked out by the piled sand, and their doors already submerged. They broke out through the thatched roofs and abandoned their homes to the howling darkness. When the storm had passed, all was lost, homes and fields and centuries of cultivation, beneath a barren wilderness: In subsequent centuries, wind erosion occasionally uncovered the branches of trees, which struggled back into leaf until the remorseless sand closed over them again. The chimneys of the mansion emerged from the sands during the eighteenth century. A photograph exists of the furrows that were being ploughed when the storm struck, over two hundred years before the picture. The abandoned plough is now in Nairn museum. These were fleeting glimpses; the estate was buried, in some places, over one hundred feet deep. Culbin remained a desert until the 1920's, when The Forestry Commission bought the Land and planted it with Scots and Corsican Pine. The trees thrived and stabilised the Dune system with their roots. Now the vegetation beneath the trees has grown, and the visitor walks on grassy hills that are the frozen dunes, some up to thirty metres high, with the lost farms of 1694 still enclosed within them.

Kinnaird petitioned Parliament to try to get relief from taxation, and joined an enterprise that had begun to found a Scottish colony on the Isthmus of Panama, called the "Darien venture." The failure of this great enterprise was to cost Kinnaird his life, and make the Union of England and Scotland an economic necessity.

5. FINDHORN, GLENBUCHAT, CULLODEN

Today's Findhorn is the third village of that name. The sea has redrawn the coast so radically that one of the earlier sites is a mile offshore. Sunlight shimmers on the water and a soft haze blurs the boundaries of sea and sky, making a huge backdrop to the little village with its crow-stepped gables and narrow lanes. They lead the wanderer down to the quay on Findhorn Bay, an inlet of the sea shaped like a gigantic teardrop among high sand dunes. At the Southern end of the bay the Muckle Burn and the Findhorn River meet among broad banks of mud and sand. The bay is a nature reserve, and a famous site for bird watching. For centuries it provided shelter for the little cobbles used by the fishermen. The village was famous for a type of smoked fish, and their peat smoking technique became a jealously guarded trade secret. Local merchants sold the fish throughout Britain, and smuggled letters in the packages as a lucrative by-product. Postal services were an expensive royal monopoly, charging by the mile. The smugglers must have delivered some aromatic letters.

It wasn't only mail that was smuggled. Local boatmen lost a hoard of silks, spices and tea when the sands overwhelmed Culbin. Hundreds of people came to dig for it, but it was never found. Even the most pious of the Brodies of Brodie managed a little "Free Trade" on the side. One Provost of Forres fled the country when a cargo of uncustomed goods came to the attention of the Revenue. He was storing them in a warehouse belonging to Brodie of Lethen. There was a remarkable system in Nairn for warning smugglers of the presence of the revenue men. When a cargo was ready to be delivered, a boy would be sent to the tobacconist in the town with a snuff box. If "the coast was clear" the snuffbox would be returned full. If the excise men were about, it was sent back half-empty. In this way messages could be passed like snuff, under the noses of the excise. There were Brodie Clansmen among the organisers and perpetrators of the trade, of course. We read of George Brodie, master of the Sloop *Despatch*, smuggling Gin, Silk and Lace, and William Brodie of the Brig *Charming Baby*, running uncustomed red wine. Unfortunately we read of them in informer's letters to the excise. Let's hope that they got through.

East of the Findhorn the level sands stretch away, empty and remote, against the cold, crystal-clear waters of the Firth. The beach is bounded by sea-piled boulders, mostly grey, but with some glittering pastel coloured quartz among them, yellows, blues, green and white, like natural Easter eggs. The ribs of a wooden wreck show through the sand at the water's edge, and an ancient anchor with a broken fluke lies nearby, telling a common tale of the sailing trade along this coast. So much has improved. Findhorn today is a favourite venue for yachting and water sports, sailing schools and regattas adding to the charms of the summer scene. It is a long way from the huddle of fishermen's huts that were burned by Montrose and Huntly.

Across the bay we see the deep green of the Culbin forest. The dry and sheltered terrain has become a garden again, of a very different kind to that which Kinnaird knew. Now more than five hundred species of wild flower grow in Culbin, and numerous wild animals make their home among the pines. Badgers, otters, wildcats, roe deer and red squirrels live among the trees. Even the long endangered Pine Marten breeds successfully there. Seals and wild birds colonise the shore. Dolphins live in the Firth. Paths and cycle ways make the whole forest and dune system accessible. The whole area is incomparable as a holiday destination, with it's summer beaches, romantic castles, mountain scenery, fishing, whisky distilleries, highland games, hill walking, skiing, bird watching, Loch monsters, good food; Scotland today is charming.

It was not so in the days of William III. Between 1695 and 1699 there were four years of serious scarcity followed by a murrain among the cattle. In some parts of the country between a third and half of the population died or emigrated. There are many accounts of the tragedies of famine. Stories of unburied corpses by the roadside; of people, faint with hunger, dragging thebodies of their loved ones to the kirkyard to plead for a Christian burial. The climate of Scotland always kept the agricultural poor on the edge of catastrophe. It was during these darkest days that the Scottish Parliament decided to seek prosperity through trade, by founding a colony.

The original concept was brilliant. The Scottish colony would settle the lands of Darien, the southern part of the Isthmus of Panama, where the canal is today. They would set up porterage routes across the thirty-mile wide peninsula, and build harbours on either side. All the shipping that plied the notorious Cape Horn route from the Pacific to the Atlantic would use Darien instead. Once the trade became established, a canal would be dug to link the two oceans. Scotland would control one of the world's major trade routes, and the whole country would benefit. Of course, Spain had a notional claim on the territory, but they had never actually settled it, so the Scots Parliament thought that they could be dealt with diplomatically. The King supported the venture, at least at the beginning. It was only when the Scots started raising the Capital that English Trade interests, especially the East India Company, tried to get the venture stopped. The English Parliament supported its trade. They passed a law that made it treason for English subjects to invest in the Darien venture.

Britain was one Kingdom under William III, albeit with two Parliaments. A law that so favoured the trade of one part of the Kingdom over the other made no sense in Scotland, and left a great legacy of bitterness. Investment was thrown open to all the people of Scotland, eventually raising £400,000, equivalent to the entire coinage of the realm. It went for nothing. The English Parliament forbade their colonies in Virginia to trade with the Scots. Fever decimated the infant colony. The Spaniards attacked while the English fleet stood by and watched without intervening. 2,000 people perished in the Darien fiasco. Kinnaird of Culbin, trying to restore the fortunes of his drowned estate, was one of them. James and Mary Brodie did what they could to help his widow, who lived on in the wreckage of her home.

The failure of the Darien venture brought Scotland to the edge of bankruptcy, and made Union with England seem inevitable, at least to those in power. Certainly the English, at war with France, feared that an independent Scotland could become an enemy base. Bullying and bribery were used to force the Union on the Scots. During the debate the Brodies in Parliament are reported in being interested in the improvements in trade that political union would bring, and in virtually nothing else. Unromantic as this seems, a large part of the Scottish population was starving, and there was nothing to be done, with the technology of the time, to improve agriculture. Union would remove the customs barriers to trade with England, and help the country to feed itself. This shows a higher patriotism than the tub thumping Nationalism of the Edinburgh mob.

Local superstition soon invented legends to explain the curse of the Culbin Estate. The same wagging tongues told a story of a curse on James and Mary. James, it was said, had offered one of the Forres "Witches" a new gown to induce her to confess. When she accepted his offer, he had her burned. Now, James had attended the trials of the witches, and he was old enough to have taken part in those of 1662. But there was no need of bribery to bring the women to confession, and the story is certainly gossip, made up after the event. The "Witches curse" on Brodie, which must have been told around many a peat fire, was that no male heir to the estate would ever be born in the house. The story probably grew from the fact that James and Mary had nine children in their long and happy marriage, all girls. All of them made good marriages, and the fifth daughter, Emilia, married her second cousin George Brodie of Asleisk, a grandson of the 14th Brodie and the nearest male heir. When James and Mary passed away within a few days of each other in 1708, George became the 17th Brodie of Brodie. He inherited the estate at the beginning of the most famous and tragic period of Scotland's history, the time of the Jacobite rebellions.

Queen Anne, a sister of Queen Mary and the daughter of James VII, had succeeded King William in 1702. She had witnessed the religious persecutions of her father's reign and had been appalled by them, eventually turning her back on the exiled King. She was also the half sister to the unwanted "Pretender" to the Throne, James Francis Edward, who lived in France and styled himself "James VIII." The Old Pretender was an embarrassment to the English Government, being the direct male heir to the Throne, but unacceptable to the majority of the British people both North and South of the Border. He seems to have been a nice enough man, if morose, but he was a Catholic, and owed everything to the French Court. Britain did not want the religious wars and persecutions to start again. Anne was a (Protestant) Stuart of course, and if she had produced an heir the problem would have been solved, but the unfortunate woman outlived thirteen children and died childless. She was ill for a long time before her death, and uncertainty over her successor led to a fundamental realignment in British Politics.

First the consolidation of Crown and Parliament by the Union. This removed the fear of a Stuart comeback in the North turning Scotland into a French client state. Political opinion in the joint Parliament divided between the Whigs, who supported the Protestant succession and the Tories, who were associated with the Jacobites, the movement to put the Pretender on the Throne of Great Britain. The Brodies were staunch Whigs, part of a web of parliamentary patronage led by the Duke of Argyll and his brother, the Earl of Islay. Both were Campbells, of course, and virtually monarchs in their own right, with thousands of armed men available for service and a sound infrastructure of minor gentry to mobilise and lead them. Even the Crown had to show respect. When Queen Anne, in a fit of temper, told the Duke of Argyll that she would make Scotland into a hunting ground, he replied smartly: *"Very well Madam, I will go and prepare my hounds. "*

The Stuarts had beheaded two Dukes of Argyll, so their Campbell successors were understandably confirmed Whigs. The Brodies were wholly committed to the Protestant succession of the Crown. Brodie family members and their kin fought for Queen Anne on the fields of Flanders. There is a letter written after the Battle of Malplaquet among the papers of Forbes of Culloden. It tells us something of Service overseas in the days of Marlborough:

"We have seventeen officers killed and wounded and one hundred and seventeen private men. Our Colonel was killed, our Major and the first three Captains wounded... seven subalterns wounded, most of which can not recover...and except poor Farquhar and Brodie who are wounded, not two more Captains alive..."

While loyal Scots fought and died on the battlefields of Europe, the Pretender sought to use their enemies to restore his throne. The Royal Navy and the British weather defeated his early attempts, by respectively battering and scattering the French ships, and sending them home again. Much of the support for the Pretender's cause came from the traditionally disaffected Clans in the Highlands and Islands, and from the Gordons. Argyll and his 4000 Campbell swords dominated the anti-Jacobite coalition at the centre of Scotland. The Mackays, the Ross and Monroe men North of the Black Isle and, less certainly, the Frasers from the lands around Loch Ness supported them. The smaller houses of Rose of Kilravock, Forbes of Culloden and the Brodies of Moray once again formed a wedge between the Gordons in the East and the Jacobite Clans, dominated by the Macdonalds, of the West. Of course, these "Clan loyalties" were those of the leaders, and individuals from all the names of Scotland were to be found in both camps. Rose of Clava and even old Sir Hugh Campbell of Cawdor came out for the Jacobites in the ' 15, and there were at least two Brodies among the Jacobite officers of the '45. But not the Laird of Brodie. When general disillusion with the union made a Jacobite rising seem likely, George Brodie and his brother James, who had been wounded at Malplaquet, trained with a private militia in Edinburgh. Being short of weapons for their militia, they arranged to have an assortment stolen from Edinburgh Castle armouries by one Sergeant Scott, and smuggled out by his wife. George passed away shortly before the 1715 rebellion and was succeeded by his son, James, the 18th Brodie of that Ilk.

Perhaps we should step aside from the chronology of events to discuss "Clans" in general. The great Clans, in numerical terms, were those on lands that had been taken into ownership by the Norman incomers, starting about the time that Adam de Gourdon defeated Macbeth at Lumphanon. The tenants of these vast estates took the name of their master, and the Celtic tradition of kinship (Kindness) sustained the bond, which was convenient for both. The legal form of "Heritable Jurisdiction" meant that the head of the Clan had legal powers of life and death over his people. Many made full use of their powers, ruling their lands like oriental potentates and dispensing cruel, arbitrary and summary "justice." It is unlikely that most bearers of the great names of Scotland have any more links with the progenitors of their clans than descent from their tenants. This is not the case at Brodie, where the family were established long before the Normans arrived. The Brodies were, and are, a family in the true sense, and a Clan in the oldest meaning of the word (four or more generations from a common ancestor). In the time we are speaking of now the main family had divided in to a dozen or so landed houses, and very many tenant farms and landless families, scattered over the north-east. Many will already have left to seek their fortunes in Canada or America. Many will have perished in battle, or in the fever-ridden swamps of Darien. Others will have become traders, farmers or fighting men in Poland or Scandinavia. There are some 5,600 Brodie households listed worldwide in a recent compilation. It is probable that most if not all are related by blood to Malcolm, the Thane of Brodie in 1285.

To go back to events prior to the 1715 rebellion, the lands either side of Loch Ness were dominated at that time by Clan Fraser. Their Chief, Simon Fraser of Lovat, was a vivid character, almost a caricature of The Highland Chief, with all the qualities and conceits that the title suggests. Jacobite apologists remember him as "Lovat of the '45", but in truth, he was loyal to no one but himself, and his rabid egoism cost a lot of good men's lives. Fraser had come into his lands by kidnapping and raping the lady owner, subsequently dumping her when his aim had been achieved. He hired a broken-down priest to marry them first, and had a bagpipe player playing throughout to drown the lady's screams. He spent the rest of his life dodging the retribution of the Atholl family, to which she belonged, and in staying ahead of the law. Having become chief of his clan, Fraser made full use of it's privileges. He squeezed his tenants for every penny he could get from them, and used his powers 'of pit and gallows' to keep them in line. One visitor to his estate saw six men hung by their heels from the trees in the grounds. Fraser postured interminably about his honour and nobility, although he was utterly devoid of both. He would challenge someone to a duel for some imagined slight, and then grovel an apology before they met. He once secretly hired armed men to break up a duel that he had called. Everyone knew or guessed the truth, but the seconds quarreled over the affair. They killed each other in a real duel, while Fraser slipped away.

Before the 1715 rebellion, Simon Fraser visited the French court and laid on the flattery to the old pretender. While he was there, he claimed to be a Frenchman because the Clan took its name from the Norman Frasiers. Having secured promises of wealth and honour from the threadbare Stuart, he promised to raise all Scotland in rebellion for him. He was playing the loyal Hanoverian at home of course, for every penny that he could make from it. The French were very happy to back their Stuart puppet, and they financed an expeditionary force to land on the Scottish coast in the late summer of 1715. The French Invasion, supported by the Jacobite Rising, would carry the Stuart to his Throne. Unfortunately for the pretender, the French King died five days before the invasion fleet was due to sail. Unfortunately for Scotland, the pretender postponed his invasion but omitted telling his supporters. The Jacobite leader was the Earl of Mar, an elderly politician known as "Bobbing John" for his alacrity in changing sides. When the Jacobites raised the "Standard on the Braes o' Mar" on August 26th, 1715, the knob at the top of the pole fell off. Twelve thousand brave and warlike Highlanders joined the Rebellion, and between them and the border there was only Argyll with two thousand Campbells. Too many for bobbing John. He marched on Perth, took the town, and stayed there. Back in Brodie Castle, James had received a threatening letter from the Marquis of Huntly, demanding his arms and horses. He was supposed to get a receipt for them from the Laird of Altyre. The Brodie must have felt that he had travelled backwards in time as these familiar enemies made their demands. The Gordon's letter went on to say that if Brodie refused the demand his house would be battered down, his tenants razed, his crops destroyed and everyone killed. Brodie sent back a civil reply, saying that, in these troubled times, he clearly needed his weapons for his own defence, and his horses for himself and his followers, and therefore begged to be excused. Brodie's home was still the stark defensive tower of the bloodfeud days, if a little more comfortable within. The Gordon may have been considering this, for he sent a more conciliatory second note, promising his protection if the Brodie would comply. James replied politely that he would rather suffer in a good cause than be protected by a rebel, which sent Huntly scouring the countryside for cannon. Finding none big enough to batter down the house, he gave over and took his Gordons South to join Bobbing John. He sent several of The Brodie's neighbours and kinsmen who had, alas, joined the rebellion, to try to reason or frighten him into compliance. James admitted them all, and politely refused bribery and threats alike. He may have given them something to think on in return, such as the penalties for treason in the year 1715. Loyalty had its price, too. The Brodie was obliged to supply grain and meal from his estate to the forces of Government, at his own expense, and to feed 1200 Government troops as they passed through on their way to Elgin, and again when they returned. He also had to maintain a garrison at Brodie for two months, which at least made Gordon reprisals less likely.

At this late stage of the rebellion, Simon Fraser arrived back from France, where he had been swearing his loyalty to the pretender. Once back in Scotland, he quickly saw which way the wind was blowing, and became a Hanoverian again. He took three hundred of his Fraser Clansmen and occupied Inverness, where he proclaimed himself the *Saviour of the North*. The Frasers that had joined the rebellion deserted and made their way home. The Jacobite army had clashed with Argyll's much smaller force at Sherrifmuir, and had withdrawn back to Perth after an indecisive battle. The rebellion was spent. Large numbers of highlanders deserted. Then the pretender finally arrived.

He was a public relations disaster for his own cause. Morose, pompous, and with a gift for saying the wrong thing, he infuriated the chiefs who had risked everything for his cause, *"...we saw nothing in him that looked like spirit...some asked if he could speak..."* when he did speak it was to make such inspiring remarks as *"...my whole life...has been a constant series of misfortunes"* ...soon the rebels were describing their "King" as "Old Mister Melancholy". As reinforcements arrived for Argyll's army to the South, the Highlanders packed up their loot and went home. Only the winter snows in the passes held the Campbells back, and as the thaw began so did their advance. The pretender promptly deserted, and went home to France. He wrote a letter to his abandoned army saying that he was doing it for their own good. His generosity led to hundreds of clansmen being sent as slaves to the West Indies, nineteen estates confiscated, and the beheading of two of the more prominent leaders. This was quite mild retribution by the standards of the time. It reflected the Government's relief that the long awaited rebellion had proved a damp squib. An act of Parliament was passed to disarm the Clans, but it was enforced in a half-hearted way. Broken and useless weapons were imported from abroad to be handed in to the authorities, while the real weapons were carefully stored for future use.

James Brodie, the 18th Laird, lived to enjoy his inheritance for only five years. During this time his younger Brother Alexander wrote a famous letter to him, still kept at Brodie. In it he explained a theory of the stewardship of great estates, put forward by a writer called Sir Richard Bulstrode in a book of essays published in 1715. He quoted the theory of four types of actor in the theatre of great families. They were The *Beginner*, the *Advancer*, the *Continuer* and the *Ruiner*. Within three years of the letter, James died, and Alexander, one of the Great Figures of Brodie history, became the 19th Laird of Brodie.

There was another attempt by the Jacobites in 1719, this time using Spanish regular troops to support the Clansmen. Simon Fraser, who had been made governor of Inverness Castle by a grateful Government, wrote to the rebels offering to surrender. To his chagrin, they were defeated before they could take up his offer, and the proof of his treachery was still with them. He continued as Governor of Inverness, but remained in contact with the pretenders' "court," which was now based in Rome. He was pardoned by the Stuart for turning his coat, and promoted to cloud cuckoo rank and honours, to be enjoyed when the Stuarts returned to the throne. He was very active posing as a Whig in local politics, which brought him into conflict with the Brodie.

Alexander had succeeded his brother in 1720, and became Member of Parliament for Elgin the same year. He maintained the Whig tradition of the family and was a staunch supporter of the Government. His political group were called the *Argathelians*, the followers of the Duke of Argyll. He was rewarded by promotion to the office of Lord Lyon in 1727. This office put him at the head of the court that decided questions of rank and honour in Scotland. In 1724 he was married to Mary Sleigh, a beautiful, clever and light-hearted woman, the daughter of Major Sleigh of the British Army. Mary was a famous beauty, known throughout Scotland by a cheery song describing her walking the Royal Mile at Edinburgh, the envy and admiration of all. Time has changed the name in the song from Mary Sleigh to "Mally Lee" but the delight in her beauty and vivacity shines out from the text:

The dance gaed through the palace hall, a comely sight to see:

And none was there so bright or braw as bonny Mally Lee

And some had jewels in their hair, like stars mid clouds did shine,

Yet Mally did surpass them all wi' but her glancin eyne

It was Mary's fate to be celebrated in song, poem, and prose, not only for her beauty, but also for her astute business sense and care for her tenants. Allen Ramsey, the foremost Scottish poet of the time, produced a distinguished work to celebrate the marriage. An extract tells us the spirit of the occasion:

In your accomplished mate, young Thane

Without reserve ye may rejoice

The Heavens your happiness sustain

And all that think, admire your choice;

Around your treasure encircling arms entwine

Be all thy pleasures hers and hers be thine

Rejoice dear Mary, in thy youth,

The first of his brave ancient clan

Whose soul delights in love and truth

And viewed in every light, a man

To whom the fates with liberal hand have given

Good sense, true honour and a temper even

Alexander and Mary were very active in improving conditions for their tenants and in beautifying the Castle grounds. The word improvement has become sinister in Scotland's history, often being used to denote mass evictions, but Mary's seem to have been benign. She had the grounds of Brodie landscaped and adorned with fine carriageways lined with trees. She arranged craft training for local women, raised flax on the estate and had a flax mill built to process it. She introduced new agricultural methods to improve productivity. With frequent trips to London when her husband was attending Parliament, and social contact there with landed gentry from all over Britain, she was ideally placed to absorb new ideas in agriculture. Potatoes were grown for the first time in the area, and turnips for winter feed. Improved methods of ploughing displaced the inefficient four horse monsters. The old Runrig (strip farming) techniques were abandoned in favour of field enclosures and crop rotation. In Forres, a board of manufactories was set up to encourage local industry. The house too was brought up to date. New marble fireplaces were installed, a straight staircase replaced the old (but easily defended) circular one, the battlements and turrets were removed from the tower, and a spectacular ornamental plaster ceiling was installed in the Laird's Chamber (now the red drawing room). Brodie was rapidly turning into a stately home. There is a picture of Alexander hanging in the castle to this day. It shows a stout, bewigged, cheerful looking man with a florid eighteenth Century countenance, more like an English Squire than a Scottish Chief. The eyes have a thoughtful, appraising look, suggesting a man who would think carefully before speaking or acting. This impression, alas, is not borne out by his history.

Argyll's brother Islay and Duncan Forbes of Culloden managed the political interests of the Duke on a day to day basis. Forbes was Lord President of Scotland, one of the most influential men in the land, and Brodie had a close working relationship with him. They manipulated events and elections in the Governments interests, and this sometimes brought them into conflict. Forbes was a deep manipulator, willing to negotiate secretly with Jacobites and Hanoverians alike, to buy off dangerous enemies and to suppress evidence when necessary to acquire political leverage. Brodie seems to have been a bluff and straightforward man, quite willing to go on the offensive when he thought some political action to be out of order. He quarreled furiously with Forbes, (which did his own career immeasurable harm). Alexander's letters speak of Duncan Forbes *"...and his Popish Jacobite adherents"* which shows more loyalty to the Crown than understanding of political expediency. Forbes kept his relations with the Jacobite Clan leaders friendly so that he could exert influence on them. This probably saved Scotland for the Crown in 1745. Alexander never seems to have understood. He even managed to fall out with Brodie of Lethen over some trivial affair *"With his Jacobite friend Duncan."* Mary Sleigh tried her best to mend relations, especially with Duncan Forbes. Some of her letters are preserved among the Culloden papers, expressing her dismay at the coldness between them. Forbes replied courteously that he still held Mary (Who he referred to as The Lyoness) in high esteem, but that he could not be reconciled to the Lyon. In the event it was danger to the Kingdom rather than the heartfelt protestations of a Lady that brought the two back together.

Brodie got into a row with Fraser of Lovat over the Nairn elections of 1737. Fraser was playing his usual double game, publicly supporting Islay's candidate while secretly working for his opponent. Brodie confronted Fraser with his treachery, and told him Islay would know of it. Fraser retorted that Islay would not drop him *"...for all the Brodies on earth together with all the devils in hell..."* Fraser, ever the windbag, told anyone who would listen that he intended a duel with the Lord Lyon after the election, but, as usual, he never came up to the scratch. His true feelings were revealed by his statement that he would fight Brodie even *"if I had to crawl across the desert to fight a Lyon as stout (brave) as any in Arabia"* Well, crawling was ever one of Frasers accomplishments, whether to Islay or to the pantomime court of the pretender. Brodie didn't need to posture.

They were distantly related by marriage. Fraser's second wife, Margaret Grant, was the daughter of Ludovick Grant (Chief of the Speyside Grants and a major power in the region) and Janet Brodie of Lethen. Margaret bore Simon Fraser two sons. The firstborn son, (also called Simon) had King George for his Godfather. He fought against the Crown in 1745, and yet lived on to become a General in the British Army. Alexander Brodie went to some lengths after the '45 to ensure that the younger

Simon, the Master of Lovat, survived. Perhaps he did so for the memory of Margaret. She died giving birth to Fraser's second son, who grew up, without her, into a hard drinking rascal. Fraser married a third time, to Primrose Campbell. It was a politically useful match for Fraser, but it was a nightmare for Primrose.

Before their quarrel, Fraser had sought Brodie's patronage and had referred to him as "The Squire" Fraser gossiped in a letter that the Brodies had spent £15,000 sterling on balls, plays, quadrilles, feasts, and operas. Whether the sum is true or not, it suggests that the Brodies were enjoying life. *"If she was my wife"* wrote the poltroon of Lovat *"...I would give orders to sail her to the West Indies, and leave her Queen of St. Lucia, now possessed by ye polite and courteous French nation...for the Lady does understand the French very well..."* Ignoring the lascivious jealousy that drips from the poltroon's pen, Fraser knew what he was talking about. He had kidnapped his own first "wife," he had marooned the wife of Lord Grange on the Island of St. Kilda, and he kept his current wife, Primrose Campbell, naked and half- starved, locked in a room in Castle Downie. In public, however, he played the part of "Highland Gentleman loyal to the Government." When local militias were raised to patrol the highland borders, Lovat was awarded command of a company.

The Military Commander in the North at this time was General Wade. He tried to disarm the Clans, with limited success, and built some 250 miles of surfaced road to link the forts that had been built to police the highlands. A Wade Bridge was built over the Findhorn at Dulsie Bridge, a few miles South of Brodie, and is still in use today. It was believed at the time that the construction of good roads would increase commerce and bring civilising influences into the highlands. In practice, few would travel the roads without a military escort. Wade employed highlanders to help in the construction of the roads, and quickly realised their value as skilled irregular troops with priceless local knowledge and acceptability to the inhabitants. The Gaelic-speaking troops could acquire military information far beyond the capabilities of the alien redcoats. He organised them into six militia companies, and set them to work preventing cattle raiding and blackmail along the highland border. They soon became known as the Black Watch, both from their preventative duties and their dark government tartan. Three of the companies were raised by the ever-loyal Campbells, and one each by the Grants, Munroes and Frasers. The General collated the information that his militias gathered, and assessed the military strength of the highlands and the Jacobite threat. He estimated that there were 22,000 men available for military service in the area, of which 10,000 were loyal to the crown and 12,000 "Ready to rise in arms for the Pretender." His estimate of the "Loyal" highlanders included 800 or so Frasers, under the slippery Lord Lovat.

A map made by Lempriere in 1731 shows the distribution of forces. Argyll, with his 4,000 Campbell followers, dominates the southern end of the Great Glen. The Duke of Sutherland's men occupy the strategically significant Caithness coast and the Munroes, Grants, Roses and Frasers, the lynch pin area around Inverness. The Brodies were part of this Whig coalition, but their numbers were too small for Lempriere to record. To the west and north-west the ancient coalition, dominated by the Macdonalds, could muster up to eight thousand men. To the East the Gordons, one thousand or so, to the South, the Clan Chattan confederacy led by the Macpherson and Macintosh men. The militias could police the fringe areas but North and West of the Great Glen the King's writ did not run, any more than it had in the fifteenth century.

Duncan Forbes of Culloden, the Lord President, had proposed to Parliament that five thousand men of military age should be conscripted in the Highlands for service in the British Army, but the suggestion was not taken up. The Highlanders were perceived as little more than savages, unfit to wear the King's coat, and the effectiveness of their fighting methods was not appreciated in the age of military choreography. Clan leaders felt free to maintain their old anarchic ways, secure in their mountain hideaways, even as Wade built the roads for modem armies to move along. Some of the chiefs actively recruited their men for service in the armies of France, with whom Britain was at war. Government policy did nothing to allay this. Even the vital local militias were withdrawn for overseas service as the war with France progressed. The Government saved fifteen thousand pounds a year by this withdrawal, at the ultimate price of civil war and National catastrophe.

The power vacuum created by the withdrawal of the militias gave the Highland chiefs fresh opportunities for banditry. By May 1745 Alexander Brodie of Brodie, Lord Lyon of Scotland and Member of Parliament for Elgin, had to pay blackmail to Cluny Macpherson to keep the Clan Chattan men from raiding his lands. Brodie of Lethen had to intervene with Macpherson to ask him not to attack the lands around Elgin where the extortion had not yet been paid. There was a Brodie household at Spynie just north of Elgin that may have been at risk, and another at Windy Hills, near Burghead. Even the Campbells in outlying districts, had to pay or be burned out. The lives, homes and livestock of small tenant farmers had to be defended by bribery and the Caterans were making the law. Some modern historians represent these activities as an early form of insurance. They seem to me to be a well- developed form of gangsterism.

Brodie's neighbour, Fraser of Lovat, gave no outward sign that he was disaffected, and to call him Jacobite is to give him more honour than he deserves. He used the anarchy for his own gain. He stood down his militia men but continued to pocket their wages, used his Frasers to raid and harry his neighbours, and accepted Cluny Macpherson, the bandit chief of Clan Chattan, as his son in law. In 1739 General Wade stripped Fraser of his command, which sent the old poltroon into paroxysms of rage against the Government and all those (like Brodie) representing it. He vigorously pursued his contacts with the Pretenders court and sought to persuade the French to invade Scotland. His optimistic appraisals of the support such an invasion would receive impressed the French Military, and were a trigger to the National catastrophe remembered by romantics as "The Forty-five."

The French, hard pressed by the wars in their own country, decided to set fire to the Highlands with a well-equipped invasion force led by the Pretender's handsome and charismatic son, Charles Edward, (the Young Pretender). The clan chiefs were to order out their men in support of French regular troops, and together they would invade England and march on London. The King would flee or be killed, and Britain would have an absolute, Catholic, Stuart monarchy again with a French army of occupation to maintain it's authority. The Old Pretender would be brought from Rome and crowned in Westminster Abbey. The Highland banditti would be rewarded with wealth and honours and the Whig clans would be dispossessed and broken ... in the Pretender's dreams ... in truth, the French wanted a diversionary attack on the British mainland to force troop withdrawals from Flanders... and that was what they got.

In March 1744, a grand expedition left Dunkirk for the British coast, with sixteen ships of the line, seven frigates, and numerous transports packed with French Regular soldiers, field artillery, and stores. The Young Pretender accompanied the French Commander in Chief, fulfilling his hereditary duty as French puppet... but the Royal Navy threatened them while they were at anchor, so they cut their anchor cables. They ran for the French coast, but without anchors they couldn't help themselves when the wind got up, and they were driven ashore near Brest. Twelve ships sank - seven with all hands. The French high command lost interest in the scheme.

The Young Pretender could not stomach his disappointment. He borrowed money and fitted out a borrowed ship, the *Doutelle* of Nantes, for a private expedition. Equipped with twenty field guns, 3500 firearms, 2400 broadswords, and a rag-tag band of adventurers, the 'Bonny Prince' set sail for Scotland in June 1745. He was escorted by a French National Ship, the *Elisabeth*, 64. They were intercepted in the Channel by *Lion*, 50, which crippled the French liner and drove her back to port. She took half the Pretender's supplies and all of his artillery with her.

The *Doutelle* received some damage from the British ship's stern guns, but made good her escape and reached Eriskay in the Hebrides. Macdonald and Macleod refused to meet the Pretender and advised him to go home to France, so he continued to Moidart on the mainland. Here he cajoled and shamed the erstwhile Jacobite chiefs into supporting him, and they in turn bullied and threatened their followers into his service. Cameron of Lochiel made the position of the subordinate clansmen quite clear when he declared to the Italian upstart *"I will share the fate of my Prince ... and so will every man over whom nature or fortune has given me power."* The romantic imagery of brave highlanders answering the call of their Prince to start a civil war out of patriotic chivalry hardly bears examination. When a chief chose to fight his power of "pit and gallows" over his tenants ensured that they would do most of the fighting. Lochiel negotiated a guaranteed income equivalent to that of his estates, before he would declare for the Pretender. He played his part bravely, and survived to enjoy an income of seven hundred pounds a year in France. Of the eight hundred Cameron men that he ordered out to do the Pretender's fighting, four hundred and sixty never came back. There were no French Government pensions for their dependants.

Whig politics played a big part in determining which clans came out for the Pretender. Duncan Forbes lobbied the clan chiefs furiously to warn them of the consequences if they took part in the rising. His influence over Macleod of Harris and Macdonald of Sleat secured their neutrality. The two chiefs had sold hundreds of their people into slavery in the West Indies, but some had been rescued en route. Forbes had not prosecuted the chiefs but they knew that he could. They snubbed the Pretender and stayed at home. Forbes warned the owners of estates that had suffered forfeiture and eventual restoration after the 1715 rebellion not to risk them again. Before leaving to take his place in the British Army, Alexander Brodie wrote to Ludovick Grant suggesting that Fraser of Lovat (and thereby his 800 swords) could be bought by paying compensation for the loss of his militia company. Everywhere the Whig interest used reward and punishment to maintain, if not loyalty, at least practical neutrality among those with something to lose. This led to a simple fact of the '45, the most impoverished clans were the most 'Jacobite'.

Not all the Brodie households supported King George. There were Brodies living in Glenbuchat, thirty miles South of Elgin, who rose for the Pretender, and there may well have been more. The Glenbuchat Brodies were descendants of John Brodie, the third son of David of the Bloodfeud days. They lived deep in Gordon Country, among the Ladder Hills, close by the Tower House of their Laird, Gordon of Glenbuchat. There is a charming little poem describing the beauty of the Glen in differing seasons. An extract gives the flavour:

Glenbuchat in summer is fair,

When daisies deck the lea

When broom and wild rose scent the air

and lure the passing bee.

In those days, before the mass emigration of the nineteenth century, the Glen contained many more homes than it does today. The little estate supplied two hundred swords for the Stuart. Glenbuchat was sixty-eight years old when the rebellion began, and racked with arthritis, but he led his followers throughout the campaign. He made William Brodie of Glenbuchat his Sergeant of Horse, and together they collected men and horses for the cause. Men who refused to join the Jacobite army had their cattle killed and their thatch set on fire. All the horses of the area, including those of the Duke of Gordon, were rounded up and put into the Pretenders service, with or without their owner's permission.

Glenbuchat is remembered as one of the stars of the Stuart cause. As a young man, he had taken part in the Highland charge that destroyed the redcoats at Killiecrankie. In his forties, he had fought against the Campbells at Sherrifmuir. The failure of the '15 caused him to live at peace with the House of Hanover for a few years, but, in 1737, he sold his little estate to the Earl of Fife and went to join the Pretender at Rome. Now, as an old man, he came back to lead his people on one last campaign. King George knew his fame well. It is said that during the rebellion the King would wake in the middle of the night screaming *"Der Great Glenboggat is coming!"* and have to be soothed back to sleep like a child.

William Brodie of Glenbuchat had much to lose. He was a prominent man in the Glen, and a favourite of Earl Fife. It was his privilege to share a dram with the Earl during his annual visit to the Glen, when they would drink the health of the tenants. He had been married to Jean Brebner for seven years, and he left a baby son at home when he rode out with Glenbuchat. He wore a highland brooch on his plaid throughout the campaign, and this became a treasured family heirloom.

The time had come for all the people of the North to choose their side in the conflict. Simon Fraser chose a double game, as usual. He ordered his older son (who had been raised by Campbell tutors and was a Whig at heart) to lead his clan out for the Pretender, while he stayed home and declared himself a loyal Hanoverian. This fooled no one, and infuriated Duncan Forbes. He had done all he could to keep the Frasers out of the fight. He had enough evidence to hang the Old Fox a dozen times, including the premature letter of surrender of 1719. He resolved to use it.

In fact, Fraser had done the Pretender's cause more harm than good. In spite of all his denials, he was well known to be a leading Jacobite. His judgment was respected among the highland chiefs, and his decision to stay at home showed that he did not have enough confidence in the rebellion to gamble his estates. Many followed his example. Even so, the Pretender had a large following, and, competently led by Lord George Murray, they scattered the unprepared forces ranged against them and occupied Edinburgh. Here they dallied too long, giving the British Government time to recover from the first shock of the rising and to prepare their counter-attack. Many of the Highlanders packed up their loot and went home, well pleased with the adventure and with no inkling of what was to come. They had sown the wind.

The Pretender had an army of about 5,000 Highlanders. They were incomparable fighters, courageous to a fault but lacking in discipline and rapacious in victory. All wore the plaid and carried the targe (a small circular shield) the broadsword and the dirk (dagger). Most had muskets or pistols. Although Whig observers were sceptical *(bagpipes and bare arses ... rag¬tag and bobtail...)* they easily defeated the first army to confront them, at Prestonpans. The British General, Cope, fled so fast that he arrived in Berwick before the messengers carrying news of his defeat.

It was an ancient technique that inspired such terror among the Redcoats. Approaching in a broad line, the Highlanders would discharge their firearms, throw them down, and charge, with a blood-curdling battle cry, full speed into the enemy. They would catch the soldier's bayonet on their targe, deflect it, and strike with the broadsword. They routinely cut the throats of wounded enemies. The savagery of their appearance and the violence of their attack could demoralise even experienced regular soldiers. They had an excellent general in Lord George Murray who understood their strengths and limitations and had earned their trust. Even so, there was no realistic prospect of a tiny army of irregulars, virtually without artillery, defeating the British army decisively. Lord George could get no sense from the Pretender and his inner circle of Irish advisers. These "Irish" were not bold Feinian men come to help free Ireland... they were French descendants of Irish emigre soldiers, characterised by inadequacy and obsequious praise of the Pretender. They were jealous of Murray and flattered the Pretender until he thought himself competent, a dangerous mistake for the Stuart. He dreamed of a direct march on London, avoiding combat with the armies of Wade and Cumberland, and fantasised that the British people would rise to support him... and that was what he tried.

The Pretender lived out his fantasy for a few more months, marching down through England all the way to Derby, barely 130 miles from London. About 300 English joined the rebellion and these were left, under French officers, to garrison Carlisle. To split such a tiny force was military madness and the Highlanders deserted at an alarming rate as the march went deeper into England, but this did not deter the Pretender. We hear of him chattering gaily about the clothes that he would wear for entering London, as though the two armies of Wade and Cumberland, 18,000 veterans, would lay down their arms when the little Italian boy reached the Capital.

Atrocity stories had put England into a frenzy of fear and anger by the time the Pretender reached Derby. The rapacity of the Highlanders, and their outlandish ways, terrified those in their path. They were widely believed to be cannibals. Then a British agent, called Dudley Bradstreet, calmly told the Pretender's high command that an army of 9,000 regular soldiers was encamped on the London road. After a bitter quarrel, the Pretender turned back to Scotland. The road ahead was, in fact, undefended. Walpole wrote, as London celebrated, *"no one is afraid of a rebellion that runs away "*

The French high command had already got their diversion. Three battalions of guards and seven infantry regiments were returned from France and put under the command of William Augustus, the Duke of Cumberland. Cumberland was a hard, experienced and utterly ruthless professional soldier. He was also a member of the Royal House that the Stuarts had sought to overthrow five times, using the Highlands as their base. He had plenty of time to consider his strategy on the long pursuit northwards. He made contact with the rebel army on the road through Forres in April 1746.

In Brodie Castle, Mary had run the household while her husband was away at the war. The Earl of Loudon, a Campbell chief, led the Government militia around Inverness and Mary supplied his troops with meal from the Brodie Estates. Rebels had also helped themselves to supplies from Brodie as they passed before heading into England. Early in 1746, the retreating Jacobites were back in the district, and occupying the surrounding countryside. Brodie now had a garrison of Redcoats again. Mary was obliged to supply the soldiers and their servants with food, and to provide feed and straw for their animals. She wrote afterwards that they were extremely welcome to the best that the House could afford. Alexander's cousin, James Brodie of Spynie, had the rebels occupying his household. They robbed him of every scrap of supplies, and a year and a half's rent, and obliged him to buy in more food when they had exhausted his stores. They told his wife that when they moved on they would burn her estate and all the surrounding country. A letter survives among the Culloden papers, written at Brodie on New Year's Day 1746. It was written by Norman Macleod to Duncan Forbes, and gives a picture of the military situation at Brodie Castle.

"I am joined by Mrs Brodie and Miss Isabella in wishing you a frequent repetition of Happy New Years and that we may not be troubled with such a year as is now ended... I reviewed all our troops today, and including Loudon s detachment of 50, we are but 724...It is said that Gordon of Arochy has twixt three and four hundred men scattered around Strathbogie. These, without a considerable reinforcement, will not I think choose to visit us. "

Cumberland paused in his advance near Aberdeen. He trained his Redcoats in a technique that he had devised after studying the Highlanders' methods. This simply involved using the bayonet on the left, rather than the right hand side, to avoid the targe and strike the exposed area below the assailant's sword arm. He emphasised the use of artillery to break up the dreaded Highland charge. He had cavalry and a formidable force of Highlanders on his own side, led by the Campbells and including the Sutherlands, Mackays and Munroes. More Scots fought against the Pretender than for him, although the subsequent catastrophe scarcely reflected the fact.

The Brodie was aboard the Royal Navy sloop *Vulture* which plied between the Moray coast and the Caithness coast opposite. Lord Loudon's men had retreated ahead of the rebels until Cumberland's army could come up, intending to co-ordinate their attacks. Cumberland gave orders for them to travel by boat to Banff, and join him there. Brodie tried to get the Findhorn fishing boats taken across to them, but he was too late. The rebels had captured the boats. One misty night, they crossed the Firth in them, avoiding the Royal Navy, landed on the Dornoch shore, and routed Loudon's militia. This late flowering in the Pretenders campaign was a result of his own serious illness. While he was laid up with pneumonia, Lord George Murray had a chance to lead the campaign without interference, and for a while the rebel army gave as good as it got. Mary Sleigh still had access to a boat, and she used it to carry information to her husband, on board the *Vulture* about the rebel army's numbers and positions. An appraisal sent to the Duke of Cumberland gives a vivid picture of the days before the final battle.

"As to the present number of the rebels... before their passage into Sutherland their numbers were about 2,500 not exceeding 3,000 although they called themselves 5000. That on the 21st March by the information of Lady Brodie by a boat from the Moray Coast that came on board the Vulture Sloop, the pretender was recovered of his fever was gone back from Elgin to Inverness and had a considerable body about 2000 there about him. That all along the coast from Fochabers to Inverness they were thinly cantoned their numbers very uncertain...from the Culbin Westwards and all along the County of Moray they have carried off all the meal and grain of any kind they can find save what is necessary for their own immediate subsistence and on the Duke's advance will burn all the forage...they have done the same in the East parts of Ross without leaving the people so much seed as would sow the tenth part of their lands...Ferintosh and Ferndonald they have rendered

a complete devastation and on Monday 17th I saw sundry houses on fire above Dornoch which was done... to force the country men to take up arms. "

When Cumberland was quite ready he advanced rapidly to the Moray Firth. The rebels had retreated back towards Inverness ahead of the British cavalry, ending the ordeal of the occupied households. What must William Brodie have thought as he passed his ancestral home, knowing it to be Hanoverian? Whatever he thought, he stayed by Glenbuchat and the pretender until the very last act.

The British army passed through Forres and Brodie on 14th April, 1746. Column after column followed remorselessly through the town to the beat of drum. The Royals, Cholmondeleys, Howards, Wolfes, the Royal Scots Fusiliers, Bligh's, Sempills...a broad river of red coats, well fed, well rested, well trained and equipped. The rebels had resembled starving beggars after their long retreat North without adequate supplies, without tents, dragging a pathetic ragbag of carts and a few ill assorted cannon. Three regiments of cavalry came through, beautiful animals in the peak of condition, each bearing a well turned out rider, with red uniform, sabre and carbine. Then came the guns. Fifteen three-pounder cannon on field carriages pulled by teams of dray horses and accompanied by carts filled with powder, shot and the necessary tools of the gunner's craft. Six thousand four hundred infantrymen and two thousand four hundred horse marched by Brodie that day, to meet the Pretender's five thousand victims. Even the sea had a martial aspect, with Admiral Byng's squadron patrolling the Moray coast. The Pretender had lost weapons, money, food and soldiers intended for his army, captured or sunk by the Royal Navy.

The Pretender, holed up in Inverness, knew that the end was coming. He had become harsh and draconian in his treatment of the population, and cold in his dealings with the Highland officers. He had issued a "commission of fire and sword" to Cluny Macpherson to give a veil of legality to the clan Chattan bandit. Macpherson was to forcibly recruit all men of military age that he could find, and bum the homes and kill the cattle of any resisting.

Deserters were to be killed after a drumhead court martial. Charles was convincing himself that the loyal Scots had betrayed him, and he was preparing himself to betray his followers. The French and Irish lackeys continued to flatter him. He told them to shoot Lord George Murray... the only competent commander he had... if he showed signs of betraying him. No doubt they watched Lord George carefully. Poor Murray was still trying to save the campaign. He had scouted the area between Inverness and the Spey for a suitable ground on which to meet Cumberland's army, ground suited to the Highland method of attack and unsuitable for large troop formations and artillery. He found two suitable sites, one near Dalcross Castle and another south of the River Nairn. The Pretender, on the advice of his lackeys, turned both down and opted to draw the clans up on the flat and open ground of Drummossie Moor, in front of Duncan Forbes' home, Culloden House. Perfect for artillery and cavalry, with no cover or steep ground to favour the Highlanders. There is no justification for the Pretender's orders - they were insane. It appears he just wanted to get it over with so that he could go home.

His army was starving. They had no tents. Their commissary was so incompetent that even when grain and meal were obtained, it was left in store and not distributed to the men. He had no gunners to serve the few cannon, no cavalry. His army had survived for weeks on the guts and determination of the Highlanders, and they had been endlessly betrayed by the squabbling incompetence of the Pretender and his lackeys. As a final blow to his own side, the Pretender ordered a night attack on Cumberland's camp at Nairn. The exhausted Highlanders marched for hours through the dark before the attack was cancelled. They stumbled back to Drummossie Moor in freezing rain on the morning of April 16th 1746, the day of the Battle of Culloden.

The Highlanders were drawn up in ranks across the Moor and left standing, the sleet in their faces. William Brodie took his place with Glenbuchat's men in the centre of the second line of the rebel army. The centre of the front rank, a hundred yards in front of him, was made up of Clan Chattan men. Some of the Jacobites were singing the twentieth psalm, "Jehovah hear thee in the day, when trouble he doth send..." Over to his left were French regular troops, in blue uniforms with red facings on the lapels. To his right were the Duke of Perth's men, some Robertson's, some MacGregors, and a handful of English deserters, some still wearing their tattered red coats. There were few horses left in the rebel army, and no cavalry at all, but old Glenbuchat himself sat on a stocky grey pony before his men, hunched by age and arthritis, ready to do his duty. The Redcoats marched onto the field like a military review, formed their lines, and waited. Their artillery was set up in position without interference from the rebels, and opened fire. Perhaps Mary Sleigh, at home in Brodie, heard the cannonade echoing through the trees, watched the crows take to the air at the distant thunder. Perhaps she thought of friends and acquaintances, family and tenants, on both sides of the Moor. The last terrible act in the long tragedy of Stuart influence in Scotland was now taking place.

Cumberland used to say that a battle without a cannonade was like a dance without music. His dreadful rolling iron drumbeat played unopposed on the Highland ranks for half an hour. The clansmen begged for the order to charge, but it did not come. Eventually the charge happened when the stoic clansmen could take no more. Few reached the Redcoat lines. The popping of musketry became a continuous crackling accompaniment to the music of the guns, and the flower of Scotland withered and fell, four deep before the front rank of the British Army. Those few that reached the ranks fought like tigers until they were brought low. Some, their momentum broken by the storm of fire, stood helplessly in front of the lines and *threw stones* until they were killed. William Brodie, attempting to charge, found himself caught in a wave of retreating Cameron's and Stewarts. The Gordon charge never began. As they stood undecided in the midst of the rout, the cannon opened fire on them with grape.

The Pretender had positioned himself behind his army with a dry stone wall to protect him from the British cavalry. The Campbells had moved up unnoticed during the bombardment and thrown the wall down. The cavalry charged three abreast through the gap into the undefended rear. The Pretender fled. Seeing him go, riding from the field with his French and mock-Irish lackeys, the faithful Lord Elcho, commander of the Pretender's Life Guard, gave history his first hand knowledge of Bonny

Prince Charlie... *"There ye go, "* he shouted *"for a damned Italian coward!"*

The battle turned into rout as the cavalry rode into the broken Highland ranks, sabreing indiscriminately. Those that escaped the field knew that the rendezvous was Ruthven, on the Findhom, about fifteen miles to the south. Within a few days 4,000 clansmen had made their way there, together with most of the surviving officers, including Lord George Murray. But the Pretender did not arrive. He had stolen the money meant for the men's supplies, and fled, leaving his surviving forces to serve as bait for Cumberland's troops. We do not know how William Brodie escaped from the field of Culloden, or how he survived the journey back to his family. It is enough to know that he lived to be eighty-four years old, and raised three fine sons. Glenbuchat today is actually quieter and less developed than that which the Brodies of that time knew, but the Kirk has been preserved, and there are many Brodie graves in the Kirkyard. Glenbuchat's tower house is still there, with an inscription over the door saying *"Nothing on Earth remains but Fame."* Well, Glenbuchat's fame is undiminished, thanks largely to King George. He escaped to flee abroad, and died in poverty in Boulogne a few years later.

The day after the battle, in Fraser of Gortlueg's house, Simon Fraser of Lovat begged the Pretender to return to his army and continue the campaign, but he begged in vain. The Pretender sent his followers a little farewell message promising to return with a French army, which fooled no one. The clans dispersed, leaving the Highlands at the mercy of the Redcoats. The Pretender was kept alive for several weeks by his Highland Officers, before escaping to France. There he lived a life of drunken anticlimax. No Stuart ever threatened the British Crown again.

The aftermath of Culloden still has repercussions in Scotland today. The cold systematic brutality of the victor has earned him the historic character of "Butcher Cumberland". There is no justifying the killing of the rebel wounded, although modern authors acknowledge that the Highlanders did the same. But though the prolonged agony inflicted on the Highlands was madness, there was logic to it. The Highlands had sheltered the King's enemies for sixty years. The disaffected clans had actively recruited British subjects for the armies of her enemies. They had connived at, and led, French and Spanish armies in the invasion of British soil. Cumberland himself wrote, *"I tremble that this vile spot may still be the ruin of our island and of our family"* The Highland clans had to be tamed. This implied the utter destruction of their way of life, starting with their homes, their crops,- their livestock and their menfolk. And that is what they did. The Redcoats murdered, burned, raped, and looted until there was nothing left to brutalise. A foretaste of our own times, released on a pastoral, defenceless society.

Cumberland was immortalised by a grateful public, with Handel's March "See The Conquering Hero Comes" composed in his honour and the delicate flower, *Sweet William* named after him. Duncan Forbes tried to convince "Sweet William " that even in the aftermath of the rebellion, his soldiers should obey the law. *"The law!"* said the hero; *"I'll make a Brigade give the laws!"* And so he did, to Britain's eternal shame. Cumberland expressed his irritation with the Lord President, *"That old woman (Forbes) talked to me of humanity!"* Forbes had prevented a much larger rebellion against the triple kingdom of England, Scotland and Ireland by his indefatigable political work in 1745 preventing Jacobite sympathisers from coming out for the Pretender. He was told that his efforts had not been worth twopence. *"I thought,"* he said quietly, *"that they were worth three crowns"* Fraser of Lovat was captured on an island in Loch Morar. He was tried in London, and Alexander Brodie was involved in the preparation of evidence against him. Brodie questioned Robert Scheviz of Muirton, one of Lovat's accomplices, and persuaded him to give evidence at the trial. Scheviz later repented of his confessions:

"I was attacked from all corners to give evidence against my Lord Lovat, especially by the Lord Lyon and (Norman) Macleod. They told me it would be the greatest service done to the family of Lovat to have the old man beheaded which would save the son. "

They were right of course. The Master of Lovat, Margaret's son, was an unwilling rebel at best, while the old fox had been one step ahead of the axe for thirty years. Alexander took some pains to ensure that other near-Jacobites, including Macleod, were not prosecuted. Macleod had met the

Prince on his arrival from France, but had called him a madman to his face when he heard that the rebellion would not be supported by a French invasion. In the event, Macleod had fought against the Stuart, which made him an ally in Duncan Forbes' Scotland. Scheviz was bitter at this display of Whiggery:

"If I had been examined upon the point I could have revealed more of (Macleods) intrigues than could have hanged him and twenty Lairds. But as I apprehend he has made his peace with the ministry no questions were asked concerning him..."

Scheviz gave damning evidence against Lovat. When asked to respond he said, *"My Lords, he has said so many false and wicked things that I do not know what to ask him or where to begin. "* Lovat was found guilty of treason. Being a Peer, his sentence was death by beheading. Lesser mortals were hanged, drawn and quartered. After a lifetime of running and wheedling, the Old Fox went to his death with courage and dignity. Alexander Brodie wrote that his old antagonist had died as a Highland chief should, *"that is... not in his bed..."* Fraser's son eventually regained the family estates through military service, and rose to become a General in the British army.

6 NAIRN, CARTAGENA, EDINBURGH

James VI used to joke that he had a road in his kingdom so long that the inhabitants at one end spoke a different language from those at the other. The Gaelic speakers were highlanders of course, and the road was Nairn High Street. The invisible border between high and low lands, known as the Highland Line, seemed to pass right through Nairn. Its position was clear to Doctor Johnson when he came here with Boswell in 1773, for he remarked that *"At Nairn we may fix the verge of the Highlands, for here I first saw peat fires and heard the Erse (Gaelic) Language."* the Gaelic singing of a young girl at a spinning wheel charmed him. He thought she must be singing one of the songs of Ossian, a romantic collection of Ancient Celtic poems and stories that was very fashionable in the late eighteenth century. The misty romance of Ossian influenced people as disparate as Goethe and Napoleon, and began the romantic view of Scotland that is still marketed today. It is ironic that Britain began to idealise the heroic virtues of the Gael immediately after stamping him out like so much vermin. Nairn had a long history of ethnic tensions between the lowland Scots residents and the Highlanders. The local by-laws were full of strictures against the Gael, who the locals clearly did not find charming or romantic.

The harrying and destruction of the Gaelic way of life began immediately after the Battle of Culloden. Parties of soldiers marched on the homes of the chiefs, looted them, and burned them. All of their cattle were driven in from the hills and sold to lowland traders at Nairn, Inverness, and Forres. Any Gael found carrying a weapon was likely to be shot out of hand, even if they were coming in to surrender. The repression was applied indiscriminately. Men that had fought for the crown were thrown into prison to die of neglect and abuse. It was all very brutal and unnecessary. The rebellion had been a civil war between the British people and a French-led highland-based minority. More Scots stood with Cumberland's forces than did with the pretender. The lowland Scots were enthusiastic supporters of the disarming and neutering of the Highlands. It was the shallow, pig-ignorant petty nationalism of Cumberland's soldiery that turned the occupation into a vicious display of English Imperialism. Alexander Brodie spoke in Parliament to oppose the ban on the wearing of the Kilt. He had written to Duncan Forbes for help in developing his arguments against the ban. He also argued against the universal ban on Scots bearing arms, pointing out that the Loyal Scots were being punished as if they too were rebels. Nevertheless, the bans were enforced. Heritable Jurisdiction, the ancient powers of "Pit and Gallows" were taken away from the chiefs. Within a generation, the Chiefs started to become ordinary absentee landlords, and the old bonds of "Kindness" were broken. Of course, the main house of Brodie had supported the house of Hanover since it first arrived from Germany. Literally hundreds of Brodies must have served in the British armed forces since the Union, but few became famous. One exception was an outstandingly successful sea Captain who lived in the time of the 19th Thane, the Lord Lyon. He was David Brodie of Muiresk, and his tale is worth telling here.

David Brodie was promoted to the rank of Lieutenant in the Royal Navy in 1736, when he was 25 years of age. He had served for twelve or thirteen years when he attained that rank, it being the custom of the time to take the sons of the lesser landed gentry into the Service at age twelve, as Captain's servants. David was a younger son of Joseph Brodie of Muiresk, and a distant cousin of the Lord Lyon. From the day he joined the Navy, a man of war was his home and school. Here he learned practical seamanship, astronomy, trigonometry and geometry, perhaps the rudiments of social etiquette, and a great deal about the science of killing the King's enemies. The dizzy heights of the masts and yards and the complex web of rigging were his playground, and danger his constant childhood companion. If he misbehaved as a child he would have been bent over a gun and thrashed, with ferocious impartiality, by the boatswain. He would have to teach grown men their duty, and lead them in battle, before his voice had broken. The Navy was a hard school, but a good one for those who could endure its rigours. David Brodie thrived on it, as his later career demonstrates.

The Navy was mobilised in 1739 to avenge a curious insult to British pride. A Spanish "Guarda Costa" - coastguard - cut an ear off of the master of the "Rebecca" of Glasgow, and the Spaniards made neither apology nor reparation. *The War of Jenkin's Ear* was the result. Lieutenant Brodie reported aboard the 70-gun warship *Burford*, Admiral Vernon's flagship, as it was preparing to sail. *Burford* was part of a squadron of seven line-of- battle ships, bound for Porto Bello, Panama. Vernon was an irritable and outspoken man, popular with his men but a trial to his superiors. He had been given command of the squadron almost in expectation of failure, having irritated Parliament by claiming that a small squadron could wrest the West Indies from Spanish control. He was given the command in order to prove his point, or receive the blame if he failed. Vernon habitually wore a cloak made of "grogram," which earned him the facetious nickname "Old Grog." When he sought to reduce the amount of drunkenness in the fleet by mixing water with the men's rum, the drink became known as "grog" and its effect gave us the word "groggy", still used in Britain to describe dizziness.

Young Lieutenant Brodie must have learned a great deal from the old Admiral. Vernon was meticulous in his planning, knew his craft and his men thoroughly, and had wisdom gained in a lifetime of war at sea. When he took the squadron in to capture the three Spanish Forts defending the town of Portobello he made sure, by clear and precise orders, that every man knew exactly what he should do in the coming action. Officers were made responsible for the accuracy of each gun's fire, and no officers were to permit their men to cheer (which would distract them) *"...until they have nothing left to do...but glory in the victory..."* Brodie was given command of the Admirals Barge, which was to form part of the landing party sent to storm the "Iron Castle", the largest of the three forts.

On November 21st, 1739, at two o' clock in the afternoon, the squadron formed the line of battle and sailed under the guns of the Iron Castle. First came the *Hampton Court* of 70 guns, then the *Norwich*, 50 and the *Worcester*, 60. Next in line came the *Burford*, with the landing parties in their boats towing behind. Behind them were two further 60 gun ships, the *Strafford* and the *Princess Louisa*. The Squadron sailed in line of battle across the front of the fort, and opened fire by broadsides at two hundred yards range. It was common knowledge at this time that ships could never conquer a land fortification unaided. The heaviest sea-born guns could scarcely damage the walls of an ancient stone castle and the movement of wind and wave made it hard for fire to be concentrated on a single point to form a breech. The Castle had all the advantage of ramparts at a commanding height, furnaces to heat shot to set the fragile warships into flame and a stable platform for the gunners to aim their pieces accurately. Vernon's aim however, was not an artillery duel.

Under cover of the mighty cannonade, the launches slipped away from the *Burford* and rowed frantically for the shore. Shot sent columns of water up around the boats, small arms fire peppered them, wounding some of the rowers, but they maintained their racing pace until their keels grounded on the beach below the Iron Castle. There was a battery on the foreshore. The men scrambled up, through the crackling musket fire, and tumbled in over the breastwork. A few minutes of hard cutting and hacking forced the Spaniards to break and run. The landing party was now directly below the Castle walls, where the guns above could not depress sufficiently to reach them. A few muskets were firing from loopholes in the walls, and soldiers were hastily deployed to suppress them with concentrated musket fire. The plan called for the landing party to enter the castle, but there was no apparent way in. The lowest windows, where the muskets occasionally showed, were ten feet above the ground. Brodie briefed his men to form a human ladder below the nearest window, scrambled up on the shoulders and backs of his companions, and pitched headlong into the Iron Castle. The party formed up in the room behind the window, and moved out into the corridor. Here, in the belly of the enemy castle, their presence shocked the defenders, who broke and ran before the British cutlasses. When the governor of the Castle heard that the British were rampaging through the labyrinth beneath the ramparts, and would shortly burst out among his gun crews, he ordered his men to stop firing, and raised a white flag. The Iron Castle had fallen.

Seaman Henry Roberts wrote home to his wife:

"You know Jack Cox, my messmate, he was always a heavy arsed dog,

and sleepy headed, but he climbed the walls of the battery as nimble as a cat, and so it was with all of us...such courage and bravery I never saw before... we would have scaled to the moon if a Spaniard had been there to come at...I would have sent you some Spaniards ears as a sample but our Admiral, God bless him, was too merciful"

The Capture of Portobello brought rewards for all concerned. Ten thousand dollars were found in the vaults, and distributed as prize money among the crews. Henry Roberts was pleased at his share, and looked forward to continuing the campaign:

"Our dear admiral ordered every man some Spanish dollars to be immediately given, which is like a man of honour for I had rather 10 dollars in hand than be owed a hundred...! hope we may meet with a Guarda Costa... If I did not cut off the Captain's ears may 1 be damned. "

Vernon was given the freedom of the City of London, and a new street was named Portobello Road (now London's oldest street market) to mark the occasion. The men of the squadron enjoyed three weeks ashore in the town, carrying away sixty valuable bronze cannon, demolishing the fortifications with 122 barrels of captured gunpowder, and outraging the locals. Vernon had proved his point. The victory brought a prompt response from government, who immediately fitted out an enormous fleet, including eight regiments of soldiers, to consolidate this foothold in the Spanish territories. Before they arrived, Brodie had the satisfaction of leading his men to victory at the fort of Chagres, the second stronghold of Panama, and again in taking the Port of Bocca Chica. The small squadron, under its determined officers, went from victory to victory. The new fleet, however, was a disaster.

A total of 126 sail attacked the Spanish Port of Cartagena, and Brodie, as a Flag Lieutenant, should have been proud. But a great fleet is an unwieldy weapon, taking days of effort just to deliver orders to, cumbersome to manage, less effective than a small squadron, and, by sheer numbers of men living in cramped and unhygienic conditions, bringing a more dangerous enemy than the Spaniards. Within weeks the silent enemy had come aboard the British Ships; *"Yellow Jack... the Black Vomit... "* as troops were landed beneath Cartagena's walls, the sick list grew daily longer, and there was nothing in a sea-surgeon's armoury that could defeat it. Men died in hundreds in action at Cartagena, but they died by thousands in the sick bays of the ships. Captain John Brodie of Windyhills, David's cousin, perished in the siege. Eventually the survivors were re-embarked, and the fleet went home, defeated.

Brodie was rewarded for his part in the campaign by promotion to "Master and Commander" of the newly built Sloop of War *Merlin*. She was one of the smallest ships in the Navy. She was just 92 feet long, 26 feet wide, grossing 270 tons. She had a crew of 120, and was armed with 10 small cannon firing 6 pound cannon balls and 8 petreros, or swivel guns, which could fire one pound solid shot or a murderous hail of musket balls, of great value against enemy boarders. She was equipped with "sweeps," long oars that could be used to manoeuvre the ship in a calm, or even row her forward slowly. "Sweeping" a ship was said to be the hardest work known to man. She was cramped and uncomfortable, with barely five feet of headroom in the Captain's cabin and less further forward where the crew berthed. They were required to sling their hammocks, on a two-shift system, in spaces six feet long and 28 inches wide. The close confinement meant the rapid spread of vermin and disease when an outbreak occurred. Bad weather meant everything being soaked, sometimes for weeks at a time, with no dry clothing to change into and no hot food until conditions improved. Fresh water was rationed and rapidly spoiled in storage. Clothes and hammocks had to be washed in salt water. There was a rough plenty of salted meats and dried peas, and a prodigious ration of beer or wine, supplemented (it being the West Indies Station) by rum. A proverb of the time said of shipboard life *"He who would go to sea for his pleasure would go to hell for a pastime."*

Merlin was used for the protection of the Island traders, escorting convoys of slow and overloaded merchant ships carrying the wealth of the islands to market. The convoys were a tempting target for the French and Spanish privateers that lurked among the islands. Fast, well-armed vessels packed with men would shadow the convoys to cut off a straggler, carry her quickly by boarding, and sail her off before the escort could intercept. The private men of war were often better armed, and always more numerously manned, than the sloops used for convoy protection. Many ferocious small ship actions took place in defence of the convoys, and some resulted in naval vessels themselves becoming prizes. This was the fate of two of Brodie's contemporaries on the West Indies Station, the *Blast*, and the *Achilles*. Brodie, however, had better skills or better fortune. The little sloop with its hardened crew of Man o' War's men intercepted and captured a string of enemy vessels.

The log of the *Merlin* tells of chases almost every day. Usually the fleeing vessel would prove to be British or neutral, but would still run to avoid having men "pressed" out of her into the sloop. Several times Brodie lured in enemy warships by pretending to be a merchant vessel, or by flying French colours. When the enemy could not escape. *Merlin* showed her true colours and ran out her guns. One typical log entry tells of the capture of a small Spanish Privateer in the morning, the transfer of twenty prisoners, and the detention of an American merchant vessel in the afternoon, whose crew tried to escape by going ashore. There is nothing unusual about that days events, which happened to be the eve of the Battle of Culloden. The following day Brodie exercised his men at the great guns.

 Brodie was so successful that the Spanish fitted out two Xebecs specifically to capture him. These hybrid vessels were fast sailing, heavily armed and manned, and could ship oars, which allowed them to manoeuvre in the lightest winds. They entered Brodies' patrol area, and had soon captured two Royal Navy sloops and "shattered" a third. Brodie found them, and engaged them with the *Merlin* for more than 24 hours. They escaped, seriously damaged, and never returned to the area. Brodie chased the pair of them in the little *Merlin* until they were out of sight. Another victory against the odds cost Brodie a terrible price. During an artillery duel in which he captured two French Ships, the *Duc d'Aguilla* and *Les Rouades*, his right arm was torn off by a cannon ball. He stayed in command of *Merlin* during his treatment and convalescence, and learned to use his left hand. Brodie's log entry about the incident is laconic:

"The engagement lasted about two hours in which time we received many shot in our larboard side, several through our rigging and sails and one on our quarter by which I lost my right arm and received a great

contusion on my right side. We also had some of our men hurt... they then struck their colours... "

He was subsequently promoted again; the Rank of *Post Captain* was the ambition of every young officer in the Royal Navy, although few achieved it. As "Master and Commander" of the *Merlin* Brodie had been a Captain only while he held the command. Being made "Post" gave him the rank permanently. It was also a most significant step towards promotion to the rank of Admiral, and meant he would only be offered employment in the command of the larger "Post" vessels. Brodie's promotion brought him the temporary command of the *Canterbury*, a sixty- gun ship of the line. Transferring to her from the little *Merlin* brought new challenges, with a 1200-ton ship and 400 men to manage, and a new type of fighting. The *Canterbury* delivered more than 1000 pounds of iron with each broadside, compared to the *Merlin's* 34 pounds. She was built to stand in the "Line of Battle," the nose to tail formation of big warships that presented a wooden wall, pouring fire, to an enemy fleet. Brodie had command of the *Canterbury* at the capture of Port Louis, in 1748.

The fleet left Port Royal, with a detachment of troops, intending to assault Santiago de Cuba. The wind, however, blew stubbornly from the north and made it impossible for the ships to reach their goal. Admiral Knowles knew the importance of speed in actions of this type, and the precarious health of overcrowded ships in West Indian waters. He settled on Port Louis as a target of opportunity. With eight Ships of the line and two sloops, including the little *Merlin*, he stood south for the Spanish Main. Knowles' plan depended on the swift reduction of the fort defending the harbour. The Fort held 78 cannon and a garrison of six hundred men. He expected to find Spanish ships in the harbour, and depended on their being unprepared. Any warning would allow the Spaniards to make the harbour impregnable. On the morning of March 8th, 1748, the fleet stood into Port Louis harbour and opened fire on the fort.

As the thunder of continuous broadsides echoed around the bay, a blazing Spanish fireship drifted down towards the British line. Behind her, two other fireships were moving into position. Boarding parties were quickly deployed into boats and rowed for their lives in a storm of gunfire between the lines. Two of the boats threw grappling hooks into the leading fireship, and towed her head around until the wind could carry her safely past the fleet. Other boats boarded the other two fireships before they could be ignited, and carried them after a brief struggle. Their best hope of victory dashed, the Spanish fire languished, and eventually stopped. A messenger received the surrender of the Spanish Governor, and the fleet took possession of Fort Louis, the town, and seven ships in the harbour. The captured ships represented a considerable reward for the fighting men, who would share in their value. Among those killed in the action had been Captain James Rentone of the 60 gun *Strafford*. Admiral Knowles moved Brodie from his temporary command and made him the substantive Captain of the Strafford. While landing parties carried away the guns and burned the fort, the wind started to shift, and eventually stood fair for the assault on Cuba. Knowles re-embarked his men, and sailed north. The Spaniards however, had word of their approach, and were ready for them.

The fleet arrived before the town on April 5th, and formed into line of battle. The Senior Captain, Dent of the Plymouth, asked for and received the honoured position at the head of the line, seconded by the Admiral. It was to prove a disastrous choice. The Spanish garrison had closed the entrance to the harbour with a boom made up of massive logs chained together. Under a withering fire from the surrounding forts. Dent decided that the boom could not be broken, and drew off. The assault collapsed, and the fleet withdrew to Port Royal. Admiral Knowles charged Dent with cowardice, although he was later acquitted by a court-martial in England. Brodie's next taste of action came in October of the same year. A thrill of excitement had been added to the prospect of battle. The Spanish plate fleet was at sea, and expected at Havana. Capturing even one of the treasure ships would make every man in the fleet, even the ship's boys, rich for life. Knowles led a detachment of six ships of the line, including Brodie in the *Strafford*. The Squadron pressed north under every sail they could carry, racing for a prize of wealth beyond their wildest dreams. They reached the Tortuga Banks and set up a cordon to watch the sea to the west.

On the morning of the 30th September, a British ship hove in sight from the east, signalling, "enemy fleet in sight" by the time honoured method of letting her topsails fly. Knowles knew this could not be the treasure fleet, but he knew his duty. He ordered his ships into line of battle and stood eastwards. They sighted seven ships of the line on the morning of October 1st. They were already forming their line, ready to receive the British. As the squadron hurried towards them, the slow sailing *Warwick* and *Canterbury* were left far behind, leaving the four faster vessels to engage the seven Spaniards. The great guns fired into their opponents' hulls at barely two hundred yards range, a furious continual rolling thunder that deadened men's senses with its violence and split and rent the timber vessels under the massive impact of iron shot. The flagship, *Cornwall* received so much damage that she sagged away from the line to leeward, while her crew strove to repair her enough to bring her back into action. Brodie's *Strafford* was simultaneously engaged by two Spanish ships, both of superior force. One of them was the *Conquistadore*, which had already beaten Admiral Knowles' ship out of the line. The other was the *Africa*, of 74 guns.

As a Captain, Brodie's duty had been to train his men in seamanship and gunnery, to manage their wooden world, and to bring his ship into action. Once there, yard arm to yard arm with his country's enemies, his job was to stand and direct the fight from the most exposed position on the ship. The high state of discipline that kept the men standing to the guns during the shattering noise and horrendous experience of battle could be exemplified by their Captain, standing on the quarterdeck giving calm direction. After hours of hard pounding, the crippled *Conquistadore* struck its colours and drifted from the line, its guns silent. She sagged away to leeward, and was taken by Knowles in the crippled *Cornwall* without resistance. *Africa*, the 74, remained alongside, but its fire was slackening. Soon their guns grew more sporadic as men were called to work the sails, and the "liner" started to edge out of the line. Brodie ordered *Strafford's* men to follow her round, and maintain the bombardment. Other Spanish ships were also edging away. They were trying to run for Havana, with the Squadron hanging on grimly. The chase was described by one of the officers:

"The action was now closer and hotter than ever, and the Spaniards, being sick of it, edged away towards Havana...we bore after, almost yard arm to yard arm...we peppered them sweetly. The enemy bearing more away threw us partly astern of them... we luffed up under the Spanish vice admirals stern and gave him several broadsides which, raking him fore and aft, tore him to pieces."

Brodie later described the close of the action:

"After the Conquistador struck, the Spanish Admirals Ship, the Africa, of 74 guns, continued the action with the Strafford from three till nine, when they led him in close to the shore. The Strafford being then very much disabled, the pilot refused the charge of her any longer. After great difficulty we wore (turned) the ship and repaired the damage as well as we could in the course of the night. The next day the Cornwall and the Strafford went in with the intention of burning the Spanish Admiral's ship, but were prevented by the Spaniards setting fire to her themselves"

The shattered squadron prepared to return to the Tortuga bank to renew their watch for the plate fleet. Cut rigging had to be spliced, shot holes plugged and torn up decking relaid. Hard scrubbing with sand and stones removed the evidence where men had fallen. Over and again the ships held services on deck as they committed their dead, sewn into hammocks weighted with roundshot, into the Caribbean. As the work continued, a Spanish dispatch boat entered the bay and was snapped up by the squadron. The dispatches brought no joy to the tired victors. The war between Britain and Spain was over. The plate fleet could enter Havana.

Perhaps disappointment played a part in subsequent events. The Captains of the *Warwick* and *Canterbury* laid charges against Admiral Knowles for negligence, in that he engaged the enemy with only four ships when he could have done so with six, by waiting for them. The Captains may have hoped that a court-martial would prove to the world that they did not hang back deliberately, which would have destroyed their careers. Brodie's evidence was firmly on the side of the Admiral, maintaining that he had done his duty throughout. But courts-martial in those times were highly political, with verdicts that reflected the patronage of the contenders. The Admiral was found guilty of negligence, and Brodie never received another command. His efforts to be given another ship eventually reached the House of Commons, but were defeated there on a vote. They did lead, eventually, to improvements in the system for employing officers, but David did not live to see them. He died soon after his appeal to parliament failed, and is buried in the Abbey Church at Bath. His only child, William, became a Magistrate and never went to sea, but two of his children became naval officers. Thomas Brodie became the Captain of the Frigate *Hyperion* and Joseph a Lieutenant on the West Indies Station. Both died in service during the Napoleonic wars.

During the eighteenth century we see many of the Brodies from the landed branches of the family taking their place in the professions. Of course, the iron law of primogeniture meant that younger sons had to shift for themselves. Many of the daughters married into the aristocracy, which shows that the old name was well regarded. There are Brodie physicians, ministers, officers in the armed forces of the Crown and the Honourable East India Company. There was also a very successful cabinet-maker, who worked in the Lawnmarket in Edinburgh, whose son became the most famous Brodie in all history, although possibly for the wrong reasons.

The City of Edinburgh in the 1780's was overcrowded, smelly, teeming with people. Among the grey buildings beneath the grey sky there lived a sea of human colour. University students, artists, poets, and philosophers lived in close proximity, and social contact, with whores, thieves, beggars, and lawyers. High sandstone cliffs had forced the growing town to build upwards, and the buildings there grew taller than anywhere in Britain...without an effective sewage system. Walking in the alleys and closes at dusk one had to beware the contents of chamber pots, thrown down from the windows above. The City was famous for its intellectual life. Robert Burns gave public readings of his earthy poetry, David Hume, Adam Smith, Tobias Smollet, held forth in the Clubs and taverns. It was said that fifty men of genius lived within five minutes walk of the Market Cross. The whole city was vibrant and alive with debate. In pothouses and cafes, debating societies and low dives, strong drink and deep talk were fashionable.

William Brodie was a well-known and respected figure. He was a Deacon of the Corporation of Edinburgh Wrights and Masons, a successful businessman and a member of the City Council. He was a witty, outgoing man, and a snappy dresser. He was a direct descendent of the Brodies of Brodie. His uncle had been to the Castle to paint the Brodie, and his portrait hangs there still. William's father, Francis Brodie, had built up the cabinet making business, and had taken William in to the family firm in Brodie's Close. William was a skilled craftsman. He made an elegant library chair, that still graces the library at Brodie Castle. It can be opened out to form a set of library steps.

William diversified the family business into lock making, and worked on an improved mechanism for the "drop" of the City gallows. Those that knew William Brodie speak of his friendly and generous disposition, his kindness, and his courage. He was, however, the prototype "Doctor Jekyll", for Deacon Brodie led a double life. He secretly kept two mistresses within a few minutes walk of his house, and of each other. He was given to gambling on a heroic scale, and had found a way to finance his heavy losses. A respected pillar of the community by day, Deacon Brodie was the leader of a band of robbers and ruffians by night. Brodie had a taste for low company. He spent almost every evening at a gambling house in Fleshmarket Close, where he pursued his dissolute pleasures. Here he met three ruffians of the town, George Smith, Andrew Ainslie and John Brown. Brodie formed them into a gang of burglars, and led them on raids against the houses of the rich. The gang was successful throughout 1787. Brodie maintained his double identity by bidding his family a fond good night and going to bed early...and then slipping out of his bedroom window to join his cronies on a raid.

Early in 1778 Brodie planned a raid on the Excise House in Chessels Court, in the Canongate. Brodie had observed that the key to the court was habitually hung on a hook within the door whenever the building was open, and that there was a two-hour delay between the staff leaving in the evening and the night watchman arriving. He laid his plans accordingly. He entered the excise office by day with George Smith, and kept the clerk busy while Smith took a putty impression of the key hanging behind the door. Then Brodie thanked the clerk and left. The key made from the putty impression fitted the lock perfectly.

On the night of the raid the gang met at Smith's house. Brodie was dressed in black, carried a pistol, and was obviously in high spirits. He frequently sang snatches of a highwayman's song as the gang prepared their equipment. They agreed on their positions and warning signals. Then they slipped quietly through the dark streets to the Excise office. They discreetly followed the porter home, and then returned to the office. They opened up the outer door using the clandestine key, and then began to force the inner door using an iron coulter (part of a plough). Once in, they made their way to the cashier's office, found the strong box, and forced it open. It was full of cash. Brodie and the gang were transferring their booty into a sack when they looked up to see a stranger watching them from the door. Brodie hurriedly drew his pistol, and the stranger ran.

They could hear him raising the alarm in the street outside. They quickly gathered up their booty, and fled. The gang had all been wearing black crepe masks, and the office had been unlit, so there seemed little chance that they had been recognised. John Brown, however, was already under sentence of transportation for an earlier crime, and turned King's evidence to save his skin. Brodie fled to Amsterdam, where he easily arranged a passage to America. Before he left, he foolishly wrote letters home, including an urgent enquiry about his favourite black fighting cock. The letters were intercepted, and Brodie was arrested in Holland the day before he was due to sail for the Americas.

Brodie and Smith were tried at the High Court in Edinburgh on the 27th August 1788, before the Lord Justice Clark and the Lords Hailes, Eskgrove, Stonefield and Swinton. Brodie was familiar with the courtroom. He had sat in it as a juryman a few weeks earlier. Soldiers and militia were stationed outside the court building to control the crowd that assembled for the trial. Brodie appeared at the bar at a quarter to nine in the morning. He wore a blue coat, satin vest, fancy breeches, white silk stockings, and a cocked hat. His hair was well dressed with powder in the fashion of the time. He listened carefully to the charges, and pleaded "Not Guilty."

He stood, apparently indifferent, as first Ainslie and then Brown gave their evidence against him. His Counsel, the Dean of the Edinburgh Faculty of Law, objected to their testimony as the pair admitted their own part in the crime, and were testifying to save their own skins. The judge overruled the objection, stating that the King's Pardon had been given before the trial, making the evidence admissible. As his last hope was dashed, Brodie showed no more emotion than a disinterested spectator. The trial continued throughout the night, the evidence being concluded about one o' clock in the morning. The closing speeches and the Judge's summing up lasted a further five hours, and the jury retired to consider their verdict. It was delivered at one o' clock in the afternoon of the 28th August, to an exhausted court. Guilty, on all counts. Brodie was sentenced to hang. He was imprisoned in the Tollbooth to await execution.

What can we know of his character? The Times wrote that his crimes appeared to be rather the result of infatuation than depravity; and he seemed to be more attracted to the dexterity of pilfering, than to the profit arising from it.

"To excel in the performance of...slight of hand tricks, to be able to converse in the flash language of thieves, or to chant with spirit a song from the Beggar's Opera, was to him the highest ambition. For the month preceding his execution, he appeared to possess an undaunted resolution. "

Brodie apparently spent his last few weeks in ordering his affairs, writing to his friends, neither complaining of his fate nor preparing himself spiritually. He was impatient of the Kirk Ministers that visited him, and scornful of the psalm singing of his fellow convicts. There is a persistent legend that he was planning to escape, not before his hanging (which he called "a leap in the dark"), but after it. The one regret that he did express was that he had not followed his early inclinations and gone to sea, whereby he might have brought honour to his family. His distinguished cousin. Captain David Brodie of the Royal Navy, was in the news during 1787, when he had made his appeal to parliament. His distinguished fighting record was much discussed. William Brodie must have felt that his own audacity and courage might have found a useful outlet in command of a fighting ship. Brodie did say that he was standing on his last legs and wanted to use the time wisely. He did not say what the wisdom consisted of. Legend says that he was having a close fitting hardwood collar made by his friends at the family firm. The collar had to be thin enough to fit beneath his stock, and strong enough to withstand the constricting pressure of the noose, while transferring the weight of his body through a leather harness that he would wear beneath his clothes. For the heroic gambler, this was to be the final heroic gamble. The Times records a most painful parting:

"On the Friday before his execution, he was visited by his daughter, a fine girl of about ten years of age; and here nature and the feelings of a father were superior to every consideration, and the falling tear, which he endeavoured to suppress, gave strong proof of his sensibility-he embraced her with emotion, and blessed her with the warmest affection. "

Brodie knew that he was to be hanged on the improved apparatus of his own design, a strange irony. If there is truth in the legend of his escape, it is made more plausible by the fact that few men understood more of the mechanics of the gallows than its intended victim did, and he had calculated the loading and timings involved. Brodies last few days in prison were made less comfortable by the sound of the gallows being assembled. William said it sounded like a ship builder's yard, and seemed a lot of effort for so short a voyage. Curiously for so lusty a man, Brodie drank very little alcohol, although the supply was readily available. He spent a great deal of time discussing "funeral arrangements" with a friend. He may, in fact, have been planning his escape. The Times observed:

"The nearer the fatal moment approached the greater his resolution and fortitude appeared, without any adventitious aid, his manner of living being rather abstemious. He astonished everyone that conversed with him; and his courage and magnanimity would have rendered his name immortal, had he fallen in a good cause. "

The day before he was due to be executed, he was heard singing one of his favourite airs from "The Beggars Opera." Perhaps it had a special significance for him:

'Tis woman that seduces all mankind,

By her we first were taught the wheedling arts,

Her very eyes can cheat when most she is kind,

She tricks us of our money with our hearts.

For her, we roam by night like wolves for prey,

And practice every fraud to bribe her charms,

For suits of love, like law, are won by pay,

And beauty must be fee'd into our arms

All were astonished by his cheerful resolution. Brodie even composed a comic will for the benefit of his friends. All his assets having been seized by the Crown, he left his good breeding to one friend, his dexterity at cards to another, and his villainy to those that testified against him, promising that they would soon get a rope of their own. Late that evening, he heard the sound of the drop being tested. The crash of the falling trap echoed clearly from the cold stone walls. Brodie went to bed at eleven o' clock, and apparently slept soundly. He woke at four, and lay quiet until eight o' clock, when he rose to make ready for his appointment with the hangman. He dressed carefully in his finest clothes, and asked a visiting Minister of the Kirk to keep the praying to a minimum. Brodie climbed the scaffold, accompanied by a few friends, at two fifteen in the afternoon. He looked at the gallows, his own design, with great interest. His voice was steady. He asked the executioner not to bind his arms too tightly, as he wanted the use of his hands. Perhaps he planned to grab the rope if he survived the drop.

The execution threatened to deteriorate into farce when it was found that the rope was too short. Brodie was not perturbed by the delay. He remarked that it was a new construction, and that they would improve with practice. The Times records his last moments:

"He then adjusted the rope around his neck; put the cap on, and taking a friend who stood close to him by the hand, bade him farewell-requested that he would acquaint the world that he was still the same, and that he died like a man. The platform dropped, and he was launched into eternity, almost without a struggle."

Brodie had friends waiting below the platform. It was normal for a man being executed to have a friend or two below the drop, to pull on his legs to finish him quickly. Perhaps they were supporting his weight. When Brodie was cut down, they whisked his body away to the cabinet makers in Brodies Close. The Times concluded:

"Thus fell William Brodie, a just sacrifice to the laws of his country: and while we lament his fate, his follies and his errors...we cannot but lament how improperly those abilities were applied, which might have done honour to himself and his family. His untimely end claims the tribute of a tear; for if those who possess courage, fortitude, benevolence and humanity claim our admiration, such was William Brodie. "

Or perhaps a lone passenger, in a cloak and cocked hat, stood at the rail of a merchant ship bound for the Americas, and took a long last look at the coast of Scotland. Whatever Brodies fate, The Times need not lament. He did honour enough to his name. One Edinburgh resident, Robert Louis Stephenson, was so impressed by William that he wrote a play about him, "Deacon Brodie, A Double Life. " It is said that Stephenson's "Dr. Jekyll and Mister Hyde " took William as its prototype. Mind you, Stephenson had a pretty bizarre double life of his own, brought about by guzzling from little bottles, so we can doubt the Brodie connection for that one. The Deacon's favourite song was *"Let us Take the Road, "* the Highwayman's song from John Gay's "The Beggar s Opera. " Many recordings of it are available today, which allows us to share in his pleasure. It is stirring, roistering music, full of the joy of life and adventure, redolent with the atmosphere of flaring theatre lights, garish costumes, waxed moustaches. William Brodie loved his turbulent life.

Let us take the road! Hark, I hear the sound of coaches,

The hour of attack approaches,

To your arms brave boys and load!

See the ball I hold!

Let Chemists toil like asses, Our fire their fire surpasses

And turns our lead to gold!

7. NORTH BRITAIN, ANTIGUA, MADRAS

Drumossie Moor is a tourist attraction today. It has been restored to a treeless heather covered waste. Placards mark out the positions of the regiments during the battle. The visitor feels the chill wind over the moor, notes the deep tangle of heather that the Scots had to charge through, marvels at how close together the two sides were during the bombardment. The Scots front line must have watched every detail of the loading and firing of the cannon before them.

The sole surviving building, the old Leanach Cottage, is now an annexe of the visitor centre, displaying graphic representations of the killing ground and a sanitised Audio-visual presentation of the slaughter. Here Cumberland sat on horseback, there the McGillivrays, or the Macdonalds, or the Gordons, stood while the redcoats blasted them with hot iron. There is a stone on the moor, frosted with lichen, marking "The Well of the Dead" Dying men dragged themselves to the well to try to quench their thirst. The redcoats found them there and finished them with the bayonet. Now there is a wishing well, too. Cameras click and whirr among the grave mounds. There is a shop, a restaurant, and a picnic area. Walking the scene of the carnage and watching the audio-visual presentation takes about an hour, which is a little longer than it took to slaughter the rebel army.

It took rather longer to destroy the Clan system itself. This was achieved through a series of laws called the "Clan Acts." First an act of attainder, naming men as traitors and exempting others from the general pardon. Next, an act that made it illegal for the Scots to bear arms, and forbade the wearing of highland dress. Then an act to forfeit the estates of attainted persons to the Crown, and the Heritable Jurisdictions act to take away the temporal power of the chiefs. The ban on bagpipes as weapons of war, and on kilts, strikes the modem reader as ludicrous. Yet there was method in it. They proscribed the outward symbols of the Gael's military prowess. Defying the ban could lead to six months imprisonment for the first offence, and seven years transportation to the colonies for the second. Being forced to dress as a "Sassenach" constantly reminded the highlander of his new role. Highland soldiers of the Crown were allowed, of course, to bear arms and wear the kilt, and this was a great incentive to recruitment.

In 1756, the first two highland regiments were raised for service in the Seven years war. The Master of Lovat, Simon Fraser, raised 800 men from his forfeited estates, and led them in battle. They were a tremendous success. James Wolfe, the hero of Quebec, valued them highly for their courage, tenacity, and expendability. All together, some 12000 Scots served in Canada during the war. There they saw vast areas of good farming country, freely available, in a land where the Scots were not an occupied and despised minority. Ex-soldiers were offered grants of land, following the ancient roman principal of colonisation. Many opted to stay, and so began the greatest of Scotland's sorrows; the depopulation of the land.

All this was in the future when Alexander, the Lord Lyon, and his admirable wife Mary Sleigh returned to their real calling, the improvement of Brodie. There was the landscaping of the grounds to be resumed, and the canal and lake dug, which provided employment for their tenants as well as aesthetic satisfaction. There was the western carriageway from the castle which eventually stretched, tree lined, to the horizon. The reverend John Dunbar, of Dyke, left us an excellent picture of Mary in his contribution to Sir John Sinclair's Statistical Account of Scotland;

"This excellent Lady, who had full liberty to manage matters at home, while her husband attended several different Parliaments, had acquired liberal and comprehensive views of the benefit and mutual relations of agriculture, manufactures, and commerce. She had seen much of the world before she came here. When she first saw the situation of the country, she pitied it; she knew the value of people on an estate, and studied to make them industrious, by contriving work, and giving them wages and bread for their services. The men she employed in levelling, trenching, draining, and raising fences; and trained the women to industry by establishing a school for spinning, and for dispensing premiums. She raised quantities of flax, encouraged her tenants to

cultivate it, and built them a mill for bruising and scutching it. She enclosed and subdivided an extensive mains substantially; trained up the hedges with uncommon care, and further sheltered the enclosures with belts planted with great variety of trees. Her gardens, orchards and nurseries surpassed everything. ..From these, she was fond of providing her neighbours gratis, who had a mind to make experiments in planting. She made new roads; straightened old ones, planting them on both sides; put trees in the garden of every farmstead, and raised sylvan scenes all around her."

And so the bogs were drained, the rigs broken down, the spectre of famine exorcised by agricultural improvement. Mary could not have dreamed that her little flax mill would be one of the seeds of the great manufactories of the 19th Century. The Flax industry in Scotland was destined to become an industrial giant, and within a few years of the innovations at Brodie, the agriculture of North East Scotland was the most advanced in Europe. For the early improvers, however, change did not come quickly enough. Many were bankrupted by their efforts. When Alexander died in 1754 he left the estate with debts of over £18,000 Stirling, a colossal sum. Poor Mary Sleigh. According to Lachlan Shaw (who knew her) she knew about the supposed "witches curse" and had deliberately defied it. Her three sons were all born in the house. The two older sons, George and Samuel, died in the same year as their father. Both were in their twenties. The surviving son, Alexander, was an invalid who was to die, unmarried, within four years. Shaw gives an agonising glimpse of Mary sobbing at the door of the Kirk of Dyke. She passed over herself in 1760, at age fifty six, having outlived all of her sons and having seen the burdened estate pass to James Brodie of Spynie, Alexander's second cousin. He became the 21st Brodie of Brodie when he was just fifteen years old. Mary's daughter Emilia was married to John Macleod, the younger of Macleod, and lived in Dunvegan Castle, on Skye. She took the furniture and fittings from Brodie, following a legal dispute, leaving just an old clock and a few pictures. After the vivid, adventurous, productive and ultimately tragic time of Alexander and his Lyoness, we may imagine the bare walls, the unwanted clock ticking in the quiet house, awaiting the arrival of the new Brodie.

James came into his inheritance at a time of great social change. The little cottages with a shared strip of the mediaeval runrig, were disappearing fast. Agricultural improvement brought a higher standard of living to tenants and owners, but there were fewer of them. Landless sons had little choice but to join the army or emigrate, unless they were content to remain as poor labourers. Compensation fees to the loyal lairds for the loss of their heritable jurisdictions had led to an upsurge in fine houses being built. Successful merchants and businessmen were scrambling to buy country estates for the status that they would bring. Brodie had an ancient name and a fine estate, but he was heavily burdened with debt. This may have interfered with his plans to marry Lady Margaret Duff, the daughter of the Earl of Fife, so he took no chances. They eloped together, and "stole" a marriage. There is a piquant little letter from Margaret's brother. Lord Fife, preserved at Brodie, expressing a most civil protest at the "stolen" marriage, but wishing them a happy life together. According to George Bain's 1893 History of Nairnshire, their style of life was rather more than their limited resources could afford. In 1774, the whole of the Brodie Estates were put on the market for judicial sale. Lady Margaret's brother was now the Earl of Fife, a man of unlimited resources, and a sharp business sense. He bought the whole Estate for £31,500. He gave Brodie and all the lands west of the Findhorn to James and Margaret, while keeping those east of the Findhorn for himself He sold four of the lesser properties for £20,000, and added Monnaughty, Asleisk and Spynie to his own estate. George Bain tells us that James thereby learned wisdom in the school of adversity. Alas, his trials had barely begun.

It was about this time that Samuel Johnson and his friend and biographer Boswell passed through Forres at the beginning of their classic tour of the Highlands and Islands. They passed the gallows on the Elgin Road after dark, and Boswell called to the driver to stop, as he had a morbid fascination with such things. He walked back to get a closer look, but was horrified to see a decomposing body still hanging from it, which he had missed in his glimpse from the coach. He ran back, jumped aboard in some disarray, and told the driver to hurry on. Johnson amused himself by telling his friend eerie stories as they continued through the night. The shocking figure in the Gibbet was the highwayman Kenneth Leal, and he had already been there for two months.

They stayed that night in Forres at a house run by a Londoner called Lawson. A shame for our story really, since a Brodie ran the Crown Inn at Forres. They did not visit Brodie Castle. Boswell's father had represented the Lyon's daughter Emilia (now Lady Macleod) in the quarrel with James over the contents of Brodie. It was the following day that the Great Man and his fool performed their impromptu Macbeth on the Hard Muir, and heard the girl singing in Erse as she spun at Nairn. They dined at Fort George, but they did not stay to explore the area. They were hurrying to find curious and memorable sights in the west, then open for tourism for the first time. The post-Culloden changes and the pressures to emigrate were already evident.

"That adherence, which was lately professed by every man to the Chief of his name, has now little prevalence...and he that cannot live as he desires...listens to the tale of happy regions, where every man may have land of his own... "

Emigration was seen to be contagious:

"The accounts sent by the earliest adventurers inclined many to follow them; and whole neighbourhoods formed parties for removal, so that departure from their native country is no longer exile. They carry with them their language, opinions, popular songs, and hereditary merriment: they change nothing but their place of abode: and of that change they perceive the benefit."

They stayed for a week with the Macleods at Dunvegan. Lady Macleod (Emilia Brodie, now a widow) was especially friendly towards Boswell. He attributed her friendliness to her gratitude to his father for helping her to win her case with the Brodie. Johnson had met Lady Macleod in London, and described her as a polite and sensible woman. After their first evening at Dunvegan his opinion had been raised to *"A Fine Lady."* The pair thoroughly enjoyed their stay. While on Skye, they had lodged at several houses, including that of Flora Macdonald (famous for helping the pretender to flee). Boswell, however, said of Dunvegan that they had saved the best for last. Johnson answered *"I would have it both first and last."*

Few people have enjoyed, or endured, the full blast of Doctor Johnson's company for a whole week, but the Macleods managed it with good grace. The visitors examined the ancestral claymore of Rorie Macleod, twice the size of the modern swords, and his great bow that a strong man could scarcely bend. They noted that they had seen highland targes used for the lids of butter chums, since the disarming act. Emilia was considering a new home for the Macleods, five miles or so from Dunvegan, where a convenient house with a good garden could be established. Johnson and Boswell remonstrated against her leaving the rock.

Boswell declared himself vexed *"To find the alloy of modern refinement in a lady who had so much old family spirit. "* It was easy enough for the travelers to advocate living on the rock, since they did not have to put up with its inconvenience. Emilia must have often remembered the gardens which her mother, Mary Sleigh, had created at Brodie. They talked endlessly, the Doctor holding forth to the astonishment and delight (apparently) of everyone. Mind you, they got on to the topics of adultery, prostitution and original sin, which revealed Johnson's unconventional attitudes. Boswell noted Emilia looking startled and muttering *"This is worse than Swift."* Johnson thought nothing of lecturing mixed company on the appropriate dress for ladies in a harem. Emilia was lucky not to hear his famous assertion that the English had civilised the Scots, were currently working on the Cherokee, and would eventually get round to the orang-utans. Johnson and Boswell were always up for a new experience, and they joined in with the highland dances during their tour, which provided material for some very unkind cartoons of them when their journals were published. One dance they took part in on Skye was called "America."

"Each of the couples....successively whirls round in a circle, till all are in motion; and the dance is intended to show how emigration catches, till a whole neighbourhood is set afloat...last year when a ship sailed from Portree for America, the people on shore were almost distracted when they saw their relations go off. This year there was not a tear shed. The people on shore think that they would soon follow. This indifference is a

mortal sign for the country. "

The acute observation and precise analysis of the two friends' journals is still essential reading for anyone studying the social history of Scotland. They witnessed the gulf that was opening between the leader of the Clan and his people. They observed the pressures that forced up rents and land prices in a dizzy inflationary spiral. Above all, they described the haemorrhage of emigration that bled Scotland white for two generations before the "Clearances" even began.

Emilia's son Norman, the 23rd of Macleod, accepted a commission in Simon Fraser's regiment, and fought for the Crown during the American War of Independence. An American Privateer captured him en route, and during his period as a prisoner he made the acquaintance of George Washington. He may well have encountered his rebel kinsman, Colonel George Brodie, after whom Brodie's Mountain in Massachusetts is named. Macleod was eventually exchanged and served with the Fraser Highlanders in the Carolinas. He subsequently fought in India, commanding the British Forces at Madras opposed to Tipu Sultan, the son of the Sultan of Mysore. He took part in several very severe actions, was wounded twice, and spent a time as Tipu's prisoner. He dined with him one evening, and received a wound in the face when the Sultan took a shot at him across the table. He came through it all, attained the rank of Major General, and eventually returned to Dunvegan with £100,000 in prize money.

Other landed Brodies were trying their luck overseas. About 1760, Alexander Brodie, a younger son of Windyhills, "displeased his father" by refusing to join the army. He eventually took ship for Antigua. He prospered there, buying an estate on the island, which he nostalgically called "Windyhills." In 1766 he was married to Anne Kidder. Antigua was considered the most lenient of the West Indian slave-holding islands. Antiguan planters allowed slaves to receive religious instruction, and supported Christian missions among them. Antiguan slaves were allowed to marry. They also had the "privilege" of trial by Jury. Not much to compensate for the abomination of slavery, but humane by the standards of the time. Alexander and Anne were together for nearly forty years, and raised a large family. They lived through the time of the

American Revolution, when Antigua was attacked repeatedly from the sea, and many estates were burned. They survived hurricanes, fever, famine and drought. Their oldest son, Alexander, became the Chaplain to the Prince of Wales, the future George IV, a position that must have required considerable tact. He was Vicar of Eastbourne for nineteen years and two of his sons became pioneers in the colonies of New Zealand and Australia.

In 1775, a freak of nature wrought havoc on the coastal regions of the Laigh. The great Lisbon earthquake caused a tidal wave that swept ashore and flooded the farms at Dyke. A flock of sheep drowned in the fields. 1778 brought foul summer weather that destroyed the crops, causing widespread hardship. In 1782, there were three successive floods, followed by snow that lay deep in the fields throughout March. Nothing could be sown until May, and the summer brought six weeks of storm that destroyed the struggling crops. There was a hurricane in August and the snow returned in September. All the "improvements" could not save the harvest. Famine followed. Those that had the means to emigrate did so, whole parishes and estates leaving together. Among the emigrants were Robert Brodie, then aged 37, his wife Katie Black, and their six children. They stepped down from the ship on to the dock of New York, one year before the United States was born, and disappeared from our sight.

It was about this time that a labourer working on the rebuilding of Dyke Kirk found a hoard of ancient coins buried in the ground. The coins were contained in an earthenware pot, which he managed to keep hidden. He returned with his wife, by night, and removed it. He said nothing about his find, but sold the coins for their scrap value, forty-six pounds, and bought a farm with the proceeds. The Brodie heard of his dealings, and managed to obtain some of the coins from the smith before they were melted down. They were the oldest Scots coins then known, silver groats dating from the reign of William the Lion in the 12th Century. It was during this same rebuilding that the Pictish cross-slab was removed from the aisle of Dyke Kirk and erected in the grounds of the house at Brodie. It was put into its present position at the time of Admiral Rodney's victory over the French at Dominica in 1782, and thereby became known as "The Rodney Stone."

James and Margaret Brodie had three daughters, and a son, James, who was heir to the estate. The Brodie was described by a contemporary as:

"Well versed in astronomy, natural philosophy, botany and physic, with a variety of the most complete apparatus for each science...he is well read and a good conversationalist, with a knowledge of good wine."

James was a Fellow of the Royal Society, a systematic classifier of local plants, and a friend of the Director of Kew Gardens, who visited him at the Castle. But tragedy was to befall the family again. In February 1786, Margaret fell asleep while reading at her fireside. An ember fell from the grate on to her petticoats, and she was consumed in flames, which rapidly spread to the curtains and bed hangings. Her little daughter Charlotte woke to find the room on fire, and tried to shut herself in the cupboard. When the door would not close, she ran from the room calling for her father, mercifully not noticing the figure of her mother, already past human help, lying by the bed. James, running from his bedroom when he heard her screams, and stark naked, tried desperately to drag his wife clear of the burning room. He was burned on his hands and legs bringing her out, but it was already too late, far too late, for poor Margaret.

There are fine portraits of James and Lady Margaret at Brodie. He wears a red uniform coat with gold piping, perhaps that of his rank as Lord Lieutenant of the County of Nairn. He has a long chin, a sharp nose, and a rather bored expression. His wife's portrait is full of symbolism. Her rank may be seen from her ermine stole, her piety by the gold lace shawl that wreaths her hair like a halo. Her beauty and grace are self-evident. One dainty hand is held away from the body, the index finger pointing confidently to heaven.

Brodie had a notable visitor in 1787, the Ploughman Poet Robert Burns. He was in his first heady days of success, having recently published his first book, "Poems, Chiefly in the Scottish Dialect" with the declared intention of making enough money from the sales to emigrate. The first edition sold out rapidly, and a second followed immediately. The prospect of wealth and fame overcame his desire to emigrate, and he went on a tour of the country instead, stopping along the way at Brodie, Lethen, and Kilravock. He was a compulsive communicator, which got up some gentrified nostrils, and he was a young, handsome, well built man, which set some fans a-fluttering around Forres. He was recovering from an unhappy love affair at the time, using debauchery by way of therapy. Burns wrote in the Scots language, the idiom of the lowlands that was losing out to "genteel" English. It takes a little effort for an English reader to understand Bums, which is why he is more widely read today in Russia or Japan, where he can be read in direct translation. Burns was an acute social commentator with a dry and ready wit. He contrasted the social divisions in Scotland in his poem "The Twa Dogs, a tale." The Laird's dog describes his masters rent-day:

Poor tenant bodies, scant o' cash,

How they maun thole a factor s snash (insolence)

He 'll stamp and threaten, curse and swear,

He'll apprehend them, poind their gear (impound)

While they maun stand, wi' aspect humble, (must)

An hear it a', an 'fear an' tremble!

Burns writes sentimentally of the poor but honest Scots families, who have to work hard to stay alive, but thrive in spite of all hardships:

An' when they meet wi' sair disasters,

Like loss o' health or want o' masters,

Ye maist wad think, a wee touch langer,

An' they maun starve o' cauld and hunger,

But how it comes, I never kent yet, (knew)

They 're maistly wonderfu' contented;

An' buirdly chiels, and clever hizzies,   (lads and lasses)

Are bred in sic a way as this is.

Burns suggests that the quality of life of the poor may be better than that of the rich, who live in a state of boredom and languor:

Their days, insipid, dull an' tasteless,

Their nights, unquiet, lang an' restless.

It was heady stuff in its day, almost radical but polite and sentimental with it. None of the poor tenant bodies are ever going to fight back. Cold, hungry, abused, they are expected to be *"mostly wonderful contented."* The next generation of burly chiels and clever hussies are being bred to take their place. No wonder the emigrant trade was booming. Burns stayed at Brodie and Kilravock in the autumn of 1787. He described the Brodie in his journal as *"Truly polite, but not just the Highland cordiality."* Burns visited Lady Brae at Kildrummie during his stay. He was entertained with two Gaelic songs, sung by the beautiful and charming Miss Rose. He also met the lovely Sophia Brodie, who he found to be most agreeable and amiable. Burns, ever the romantic, found them *"Gentle and mild, the sweetest creatures on earth, and happiness to be with them."* They swore to be friends for twenty years. He called the two of them *"The fair spirits of the hill."* Sophia became, in time, Mrs. Dunbar Brodie of Burgie, of whom more later.

The Brodie had a brother, Alexander of Arnhall, later of the Burn. Elizabeth Grant of Rothiemurchus, a waspish observer of society on the Laigh in those times, said of him:

"Either himself or somebody for him had the good sense to send him with a pen to the counting house instead of with a sword to the battle field. He made a really large fortune. "

He made his fortune *"Shaking the Pagoda Tree"* in India. The British Empire was just beginning on the Sub Continent, and there were tremendous opportunities for young men with spirit. Alexander helped young James, the heir to Brodie, to become a Civil Servant in the Honourable East India Company at Madras, the first British possession on the Indian Mainland. The company had sovereign rights over a strip of land six miles long and a mile wide down the Coromandel Coast, adjoining the Kingdom of Golconda, whose name has come to symbolise the fabulous wealth of the Indies. James met his future bride, Anne Story, on the long sea voyage to the east. He wrote to his father, telling him of their forthcoming marriage and assuring him that his bride *"would not be followed by a gaggle of needy relatives."* Indeed she would not. Her father was a Colonel in the British Army. James and Anne arrived in Madras in 1791. Even their landing had an element of drama. There was no harbour at Madras in those days, and the Indiamen had to anchor offshore, clear of the high surf that beat constantly against the silver sands. They landed their passengers in native boats, sewn together with coconut fibre, that flexed and yielded to the surf in an alarming manner. The passengers, having stepped down from the comforting solidity of the teak-built Indiaman, found themselves sitting on an elevated platform in the stern of the surf boat, watching it writhe and slide like a serpent as the turbaned rowers plied their oars and a native coxswain shouted shrill orders in the maelstrom of activity. Landing at Madras was always a hair-raising experience.

Once ashore, they found themselves in a new world. The fragrances of the east combined with the stench of the river mud, the brilliant light shone down on crowded streets full of vendors and bullock carts. They saw for the first time wild dates and oranges, banyans and tamarinds, palm trees and lotus blossom. It was, in every sense, a long way from Forres. There were many Scots among their Madras contemporaries, including Major General Anderson of the Company Service. He had been raised by his half-mad mother (who had been used and abandoned by a soldier of the '45) among the ruins of Elgin Cathedral, with the ancient stone font as his cradle. He had joined the Company's service as a private soldier, and had risen through the ranks by his own guts and determination, making his fortune in the process.

There were plentiful opportunities for private trade alongside the company's business, and the Brodies soon began to prosper. They built a fine house in the Madras suburbs, which they nostalgically named "Brodie Castle." There is a faded water colour of the house at Brodie. It is a fine, two storey building in the Indian fashion, with two circular towers and a domed central building overlooking a noble sweep of staircase. The ground floor is shaded by a cloistered balcony with iron railings. The front is approached by a wide horseshoe drive, with lush tropical foliage all around. I am told that the house still exists, and is now a dancing school. James and Anne raised seven beautiful children in this idyllic setting. There were risks, of course, for the British in India. On average, only one in three of the Company's servants returned to Britain alive. During their ten years together James and Anne witnessed the war against Tipu Sultan, the vigorous expansion of British territory across virtually the whole of Southern India, and the military leadership of Arthur Wellesley, the future Duke of Wellington. James did not return from India. On October 14th, 1801, he was sailing near the bar of the St. Thome River, in Madras Bay, when the boat got into difficulties in the surf zone. The breakers picked the boat up and rolled it, and James was drowned. His children returned, or rather came for the first time, to Brodie.

There is a glorious group portrait of them in the Red Drawing Room, painted by John Opie in 1805. Seven beautiful, golden children, two boys and five girls, clustered aroimd a noble looking Newfoundland dog. The tallest of the girls, Margaret, holds her brother William, the heir to Brodie, aloft in the centre of the picture. He gazes out at the viewer with a calculating, adult gaze. He looks rather petulant and spoiled. I suppose being raised by native Ayahs on the coral strand would spoil most six-year-olds. The other children look like models of innocence and grace. They all went back to India. George became an officer in the Madras Cavalry, and died there aged twenty-four, unmarried. Margaret died unmarried in the same year, and so did their Uncle William, the brother of Alexander of Arnhall. He had been Consul at Malaga before returning to Madras. Louisa married a Captain of the Madras Engineers, and had seven children. Jane married a younger son of the Lord Chief Justice of India, and had five. Charlotte married Edward Woodcock of the Madras Civil Service, and bore him nine children. Two of their three sons went into the army, at Bengal and Madras. Isabella married a Captain of the Madras Cavalry. Their son James became a Colonel in the British Army. He fought with distinction at the Alma, Balaclava, and Inkerman, and died of his wounds following the attack on the Redan. His friends built him a monument in Dyke Church, commemorating his cheerful fortitude and devotion to his soldiers.

James' sister Margaret was married to Colquhoun Grant of Lingieston, a distinguished soldier. Grant was described as a kindly, amiable man, with all the best and brightest attributes of a Christian soldier. He served throughout the Napoleonic wars, including a period as an "exploring officer" during the Peninsular campaign. This involved him travelling behind enemy lines for days at a time, in uniform, gathering intelligence for Wellington. During one of his expeditions he was captured by the French. He escaped after being transported to France, and travelled to Paris posing as an American. He travelled part of the way sharing a carriage with a French General. He stayed in Paris for several weeks gathering intelligence, before escaping on an American ship and returning to England, via America (also at war with Great Britain), disguised as a sailor. He walked back in to Wellington's headquarters four months after his capture, having covered some eight thousand miles in disguise. Margaret accompanied her husband overseas when he commanded the 54th Foot Regiment during the first Burmese War. Both succumbed to fever, and Margaret died aboard ship on the way home. She was buried on the Island of St. Helena. Grant died at a convalescent home in France the following year. They left one son, Walter Colquhoun Grant.

There is a snapshot of Dyke at the time of the children's return preserved in Sir John Sinclair's "Statistical Account." It gives the size of the parish as 21 square miles; of which half lay buried beneath the Culbin sands. Of the remainder, some 2700 acres are used to grow com; 1200 acres are woodland, and the rest pasture and heath.

"The surface of the cultivated parts is agreeably diversified with flats and easy slopes, and beautified by the windings of running water, skirted with natural wood. There are clumps upon eminences, trees about farm-steads, gentlemen's seats finely situated, with gardens, orchards and

hedged enclosures around them, and the whole is surrounded with
thriving plantations, rising one above another, with a variety of shade
and prospect, which gives the inland parts an appearance that may be
called picturesque. "

There is sometimes a surplus of wheat, always of oats and barley. There
are field crops of peas, and the cultivation of potatoes is becoming
general. Fifteen hundred sheep and a thousand or so black cattle graze
the fields. Almost four hundred small horses are used to tow the sleds
and carts, and pull the "English" plough. There are only forty pigs in the
parish - the Scots long considered them unclean. There is a brisk trade in
salmon from the Findhorn, usually salted or pickled, but sometimes sent
fresh to London packed in ice. The Nairn and Findhorn boats bring in
Cod from the North Sea, and there is a trade in seal meat oil and skin
which values each seal carcass at four shillings. There are two Schools,
male and female. The Grammar School teaches English and writing for
1s 6d per quarter, arithmetic for 1s 8d, Latin for 2s 6d, measuring and
land-surveying for 4s 6d, Geometry for 7s 6d and book keeping for 10s
6d. The school has about forty pupils. The average wage of a labouring
man in the parish is £7 per year; his wife may earn a third of that. The
average size of families is four and a half, but there are extremes. Of the
three hundred and thirty little houses of the parish, ninety- eight have
more than six people living in them, and at least one home is inhabited
by twenty-one souls. The survey notes that the women's school is in very
poor repair, and that the population has fallen slightly since the 1780's. It
gives the reorganisation of the smaller farms into larger units as a main
cause, and argues vehemently against the improvements that are driving
people off the land. Men are also leaving for the wars. For those that
remain, the standard of living is gradually improving, and only sixty of
the fifteen hundred souls in Dyke parish are classed as poor. The survey
also notes that the number of married servants has increased of late,
which is *"very convenient for rearing up servants in succession."* Burly
chiels and bonny hussies again. The survey also gives an assessment of
the character of the People of Dyke:

"The people are, very generally, decent, quiet, and well affected to the

religion and government under which they live. They are neither addicted to a seafaring or a military life; yet the frequency of recruiting parties reconciles them, when that business is accompanied by music, mirth and drink. They can live poorly to dress neatly; but few think of laying anything up. On public occasions there are not a few who will spend what they can ill afford, in vying to be neighbour-like, with others who are either more rich, or more inconsiderate, than themselves. In general they are better fed and clothed, and have a greater variety of convenient furniture, than they had forty years ago. But the use of tea makes rather an alarming progress among many, who need a better nourishment, at less expense. "

The Brodies played their part in the French wars. James of Muiresk was taken prisoner at the Battle for Helder Point in 1799; Joseph died as a naval lieutenant at Trinidad in 1801, Thomas Brodie, the Captain of the Frigate *Hyperion*, died in 1811. Another James Brodie was on the Toulon Blockade and at the capture of the Cape of Good Hope in 1801. Twenty-five years of warfare do not seem to have had much social impact on the Laigh. Elizabeth Grant scarcely mentions the war in her detailed descriptions of life among the landowners, except as an opportunity for her father to play soldiers drilling his tenantry. The war did cause agricultural prices to rise, which gave an incentive to the Clan Chiefs who evicted their clansmen to make room for sheep. The pride in genealogy of earlier times was being debased among the landowners into a complacent and patronising self-regard. Elizabeth Grant on the Dunbar Brodies of Burgie:

"The old family of Dunbar of Burgie, said to be descended from Randolph, Earl of Moray, had dwindled down to somebody nearly as small as a bonnet Laird... Burgie was a worthy man, honest and upright and kind hearted, modest as well, for he never fancied his own merits had won him his wealthy bride; their estates joined. The Lady Burgie (Burn's fair spirit of the hill) and her elder sister. Miss Brodie of Lethen, were Co-heiresses, and all their wide lands...were held by Mr and Mrs Dunbar Brodie of Burgie, Lethen and Coulmonie during their long reign of dullness; precedence being given to the gentleman after some consideration. They lived neither at very pretty Coulmonie, nor at very

comfortable Lethen, nor even in the remains of the fine old castle of Burgie... they built for themselves the tea-canister like lodge we found them in, and placed it far from tree or shrub, or any object but the bare moor."

The moor today is beautifully cultivated, and graceful mature trees embrace the house, which still looks like a tea caddy. Sophia's cousin the Brodie passed over in 1824, and his Madras grandson, William, inherited the estate. He had spent the previous two years travelling on the continent with the Marquis and Marchioness of Huntly. William immediately embarked on some major building work. He brought in a leading architect, William Burn of Edinburgh, to repair and extend the house. It was during this period that the Lord Lyon's extravagant ceiling in the dining room was given it's wood- grain effect, and the old high hall was transformed into the red drawing room as we now know it. The blue flock wallpaper in the blue sitting room was hung at this time, and it still looks fine, in the room with the 15th Thane's strapwork ceiling. William bought several fine Dutch paintings, including the Volmarijn study, "A Philosopher and his Pupils" that is one of the glories of the house today. Unfortunately, he did not have the funds to support the outlay. He economised on the building materials, using softwood in place of oak, which created problems for his descendants. He sold many of the treasures of the house to offset the debt. Eventually, the work had to stop.

In 1838 William married an heiress called Elizabeth Baillie, from Redcastle on the Beauly Firth. Her dowry allowed the work to begin again. She is described by George Bain as *"a lady of remarkable accomplishments and distinguished character."* She was not entirely happy during the early years of their marriage. She was living in the house while the building work was going on, which must have been inconvenient. She had problems finding a good housekeeper, and she was rather scathing about her neighbours. At one point she threatened to leave, and to go and live abroad. One Clan historian has described her as *"Plain and Cantankerous."* Well, being married for your money will do that, every time. George Bain says of William:

"William Brodie of Brodie was Lord Lieutenant of Nairnshire for nearly fifty years. His singularly courteous, courtly manner, his witty, wise

sayings, and generous disposition made him a great favourite in society in London, to which he was much drawn, but latterly he loved to dwell among his own people at Brodie, where he spent many happy years. "

There is a portrait of them, from about 1845, hanging in the Castle today. They look the picture of the wealthy Victorian couple, respectable, contented, sure of their position. Their lives coincided with the most rapid period of British Imperial expansion, when the success of Britain's overseas policies made her mistress of one third of the earth's surface. Their oldest son, George, was an officer in the Royal Navy, maintaining the Pax Brittanica. Indeed, the Brodie's of Brodie had relatives and clan members in every comer of the Empire, in the mighty merchant fleet that plied the seven seas, and the battleships that protected their routes; among the horsemen riding the dusty trails of the high veldt, the redcoats bringing British values to Zululand, the railway engineers that brought steam trains to the Punjab, and among the kilted troops facing the Russians in the Crimea. A few of their stories are told in Chapter eight.

William and Elizabeth visited the "Great Exhibition" in London in 1851. The Exhibition was intended as a celebration of art and science, but drawing as it did from every comer of the world it became a celebration of the British Empire itself It was held in an enormous conservatory of cast iron and glass, dubbed "The Crystal Palace" by "Punch" magazine. The central dome of the palace was so high that three fully grown elm trees spread their boughs beneath it's canopy, and the display area enclosed by the building covered almost twenty acres. Six million people visited the exhibition in five months. The Brodies of Brodie were among them, filing past the statuary, the fountains, the edifying tableaux, the displays of optical and scientific instmments, the whole cornucopia of Victorian ingenuity and skill. They bought a beautiful dusky rose carpet there, with a pattern of leaves and trellis. It is still to be seen in the light and airy drawing room that they built at Brodie. In the centre of the great exhibition, they saw a magnificent steam train, "The Lord of the Isles" - surely that name must have had a special resonance for them - A huge green locomotive, covered with gleaming brass, fittings, the very peak of modernity. Within a few years of the Great Exhibition, the steam railway came to Brodie.

It is difficult for us to conceive the social changes that the railway brought. There had been a mail coach between Inverness and Elgin since 1812, drawn by a pair of horses and bearing a guard in Royal livery, with a brass trumpet to announce it's coming. This picturesque conveyance improved postal communications and made travel feasible for those with the money to pay, but it was an expensive and exclusive mode of travel. The railways were the first mass transit system in the modern sense, and they revolutionised trade and travel in the North. By the 1860's there were thirty trains a day leaving from Forres, and even London (eight days hard riding for the 15th Thane) was only twenty hours away. Brodie Castle had it's own station on the line from Inverness to Elgin, and from thence to every part of mainland Britain. The Laird did not need to book. He just made his way to the Castle Station and flagged down the train.

So now William and Elizabeth were living in Brodie Castle much as we know it today. The Library, with it's artfully engineered twilight, the kitchens with their gleaming ranges and copper pans, the drawing rooms with their views of the garden, were all their work, transforming the stubborn old house into an elegant mansion. Of course, the impoverished years between the death of the Lord Lyon and the marriage of William and Elizabeth had greatly reduced the contents. We may imagine it then as a glorious fabric with mundane fittings. It was augmented by a most timely inheritance.

The person to whom we owe so many of the glories of Brodie today is Alexander of Arnhall's daughter Elizabeth, the fifth and last Duchess of Gordon. Elizabeth Brodie was little more than a child when she was married to George Gordon, the Marquis of Huntly, who was twenty five years her senior. He was a distinguished soldier with a great deal of life experience. His mother, Jane, the fourth Duchess, had been a great beauty, a leader of fashion, and a close confidant of Pitt, the Prime Minister. She is described in the Dictionary of National Biography; as possessing *"indomitable pertinacity, importunity and unconventionality."* It also describes her as being coarse of speech, which is how women who spoke bluntly to pompous asses used to be described. She helped George to raise the Gordon Highlanders regiment, by going among her tenantry at the head of six pipers, wearing the regimental colours and giving a kiss and a shilling to each recruit. Three of her own daughters married Dukes and the fourth a Marquis. Her later years were unhappy. She was separated from her husband, the fourth Duke of Gordon, and led "a wandering, almost homeless, life," stopping with friends and at hotels. The Duke moved his long-established mistress and their children in to the family home at Gordonstoun. The Duchess died in a hotel in Piccadilly in April 1812. She was buried in her favourite place, Kinrara Lodge, on the Spey, and Elizabeth (Brodie) later made a garden around her grave as a tribute to her.

There is a long poem, from the Aberdeen journal of December 1813, commemorating the wedding between George Gordon and Elizabeth Brodie. An extract gives the spirit:

And now the flunkies run and ride,

As frae a bow the arrows glide

The news they spread, baith far and wide

That Brodie weds the Gordon

And on their Sunday claithes they fling

An' cags o' whisky out they bring;

For they maun drink, an' dance, an' sing

Sin 'Brodie weds the Gordon

Now Bonaparte cungered fair (conquered)

The King our brave Black Watch will spare

An' send them North to share

Wi' Brodie an' their Gordon

Their hardships a' shall be forgot

An 'peace an 'plenty be their lot

The Tyrants ta 'en!

His native spot

Now claims the noble Gordon

An pipers, gar your chanters chime

Gay blithesome teens, (tunes)

an' weel in time

To mar our mirth would be a crime

When Brodie weds the Gordon

Oh! Would old Scotland's noble race

To mix wi 'foreign folks would cease

An' aye themselves an' country grace

Like Brodie an' the Gordon

There is much more of it, in much the same vein, and if it's doggerel style is tiresome, the sentiment seems to be genuine. Elizabeth Grant describes the debut of Elizabeth, Marchioness of Huntly, nee Brodie of the Burn, in her usual compassionate way:

"There she was, like another Cinderella, in a beautiful baby phaeton drawn by four goats. The pretty animals were harnessed with red ribbons, and at every horned head there ran a little foot page, these fairy steeds being rather unruly. No sylph stepped out of this frail machine, but a stout bouncing girl, not tastefully attired, and with a pale, broad face, fair - which he never liked - and stiff - which he could not endure. At the time of her marriage she was very young, and too unformed to be shown as the bride of the fastidious Marquis, so while all the north was a blaze of bonfires in honour of the happy event, her lord carried her off abroad... "

The Minister of Alvie embarrassed everyone by making a tasteless reference in his speech to the *"Coming rejoicings connected to the happy event,"* which was never forgotten because the couple remained childless. Elizabeth's Grant's portrait of a clumsy and unrefined girl is strangely at odds with reports, including her own, of her musical talent. She loved to play Scots folk songs, and melancholy Jacobite airs. Sir Walter Scott loved to hear her play the piano, and immortalised her in *"Halidon Hill."*

Her gift creative,

New measures adds to every tune she wakes;

varying and gracing it with liquid sweetness

like the wild modulations of the lark...

Of course, by Elizabeth's day the Jacobites were considered romantic and a suitable subject for soulful tunes. She might have expressed the historic attitudes of her family better by thumping out *"The British Grenadier"* Her husband had a history of active service. He had been a prisoner of the French, was seriously wounded while fighting at the head of his regiment in Holland, and had commanded a division in the Walcheren Expedition of 1809. He had progressive views for the time. He procured commissions during the war for deserving men who happened to be the sons of servants. Elizabeth Grant was very sniffy about that, but she ultimately approved of his choice of wife:

"(Elizabeth)... was an excellent woman; she brought him a large fortune, a clear business head, good temper, and high principles. She soon set straight all that she found crooked. She was not handsome, though she had a good figure, a good skin, and beautiful hands - the Brodie face is short and broad; but she suited him, everyone liked her... and she liked me."

Their marriage got off to an adventurous start. During their tour of the continent, Bonaparte, not yet *"cungered"* embarked on his hundred day's adventure. The couple arrived in the vicinity of Waterloo the day after the Battle, when the outcome was not yet known. Elizabeth, still in her teens, saw the aftermath. Wounded soldiers, some walking, some heaped in carts, and dazed refugees choked the highway. Huntly sent her to his sister, the Duchess of Richmond, who had thrown the famous ball on the eve of the battle, while he went to visit his army colleagues. The following day they met Louis XVIII, who was being returned to his unwilling subjects at gunpoint. Elizabeth was young, but she was serious minded and observant. The wholesale slaughter, the unwanted tyrant king, and the fortunes cynically made from the sufferings of the people, all must have given her food for thought. Indeed, all of her experiences at this time were life changing. She loved her husband and her new home at Huntly Lodge, but she did not like London or her experiences of High Society. *"Revelations of unblushing vice distressed her,"* said her biographer. Well, revelations of high-class haughmagandie were all around. Her father in law's irregular household was not unusual. The Prince of Wales' debaucheries were the talk of the town. The Duke of Clarence had a large family by Mrs. Jordan. The Duke of Kent (Queen Victoria's father) lived openly with his mistress. It was all too much for Elizabeth. She preferred the clean air and wholesome feudalism of home. During a visit of Prince Leopold of Belgium, Elizabeth arranged a magnificent, if anachronistic, display of Gordon power. She accompanied her husband and the Prince to a beautiful and apparently empty hillside on their estate. At a signal from the Marquis, a thousand Gordon Clansmen rose from their hiding places in the heather and filled the glen with their cheers. The military power of the magnates had almost vanished by this time, 1817, except in their ability to raise regiments from their land for government service. But old traditions die hard, and the tenantry were still inclined to see their chief as their feudal leader. The Grants were able to mobilise seven hundred Clansmen as late as 1820, and use them to "influence" a local election.

The fourth Duke died in 1827, and Elizabeth became the fifth and last Duchess of Gordon. She was a committed evangelical Christian, and endowed several local schools and churches, including the Gordon Schools at Huntly. She sold off many of the treasures of Gordonstoun to pay for her good works, and she was careful to provide relief for the poor and pensions for her workers. She had physical courage. During a dangerous crossing of the Spey during the 1829 floods, she told a terrified fellow traveler that she "chose not to see" danger. In 1831 she was Mistress of the Robes to Queen Adelaide, the consort of King

William IV. The Queen presented her with the robe that she had worn at her Coronation, and this is now kept on display at Brodie Castle. It is the only coronation robe in private hands in Britain. Elizabeth supported the Free Church following the "Disruption" of 1843, and, like the fifteenth Thane during an earlier disruption, provided funds for the "outed" ministers. She devoted much of her time to organising prayer meetings and distributing pamphlets and tracts, constantly seeking evidence of a religious awakening in the North. Elizabeth Grant described the Duchess as being *"In the Cant of the Methodies,"* and compared her unfavourably with "Bonny Jane". She did help the Duchess to sort her famous collection of minerals, which she eventually left, along with all the treasures of the Gordons and the remainder of her fabulous fortune, to the Brodie. Among the treasures were priceless antique furniture, paintings and candelabra, and some other, poignant souvenirs of Scotland's turbulent past. Viscount Dundee's sword, from the field of Killiecrankie, and the young pretender's own broadsword, said to have been taken by Cumberland himself from the Jacobite baggage train after Culloden. They are still there, on display at Brodie Castle.

George, the eldest son and heir to Brodie, died during his father's lifetime and William, the youngest, died in a carriage accident near the Church of England Chapel at Nairn in 1865. So it was the second son, Hugh Fife Ashley Brodie, that inherited the estate when William passed over in 1873. Hugh seems to have been the model of the Victorian gentleman. George Bain describes him as:

"A man of chivalrous character, an eloquent speaker, fond of music and art, a keen sportsman, and a patron of all the manly sports...he exercised a unique influence in this district, his character inspiring admiration and affection among all classes. "

We read of Hugh "Lightly and deftly" leading the dancing at the Northern Meeting Balls, and singing Gilbert and Sullivan to an appreciative audience of 250 people in the drawing room at Brodie. He had been married since 1868 to Lady Eleanor Moreton, the daughter of the Earl of Ducie. The marriage had been celebrated at the Masons Lodge in Dyke by a diverse company of farmers, tradesmen, craftsmen and clerics, which seems to support George Bain's description of Hugh's popularity.

Hugh tried, unsuccessfully, to enter Parliament in the Conservative interest. He was described in the press as being "the right man on the wrong side " while his opponent. Sir George Macpherson Grant, was described as "the wrong man on the right side... so it is pretty evenly balanced. " The elections were pretty robust affairs, with plenty of whiskey, heckling and playful violence among the electors. Sir George had his carriage smashed and at one point his brother *"was thrown down with twenty men on top of him, all done in the most friendly spirit"*. Heaven forbid it should turn nasty. Hugh's looks and charm were said to have captured every female heart, but women did not have the vote, so Grant won the election, with a majority of 258.

During the 1880's a fruit and flower show was begun in the area, held first in Dyke and later on Brodie Green. The crowds flocked in by train and cart to see the show and enjoy the dancing and merriment that followed. Every type of fruit, flower and vegetable that was grown locally was on display, along with some exotics; a giant Scots thistle and a pot of ivy brought from the battlefield of Isandhlwana in Zululand. Lady Eleanor provided the teas and there was dancing to a Military Band from Invergordon. Young master Ian Brodie won 3rd prize for his kidney potatoes, a portent of his distinguished future in horticulture.

Hugh Brodie's health failed early in life, and in August 1889 he travelled to a sanatorium in Glion, Switzerland, for treatment. Brodie Castle was let during his absence, the tenants having the use of most of the rooms except Hugh's study, which was kept locked. On the evening of 20th September, they heard the sounds of someone moving around inside the locked rooms, papers being shuffled and a low moaning sound. Shortly afterwards they heard that Hugh had died in Switzerland. He was just 49 years old. His body was returned to be laid in the tomb of his ancestors in Dyke Church, and his son Ian became the 24th Laird of Brodie.

Ian was married to Violet Hope, of Rosehaugh in the Black Isle. She was small, dark haired and very pretty. She was a gifted collector of paintings. Many of her acquisitions increased in value a hundred times during her lifetime. Her critical method could be quite physical. She once cut up a painting in order to frame the only element of it that she liked (a dog) and discarded the rest. The dog, a Landseer, still hangs in the Library at Brodie.

Ian Brodie of Brodie served with the Lovat Scouts during the Boer War. There is a photograph of him in the official history, looking dashing but businesslike in his bush hat and khaki uniform. He saw a great deal of bitter fighting before returning home after being severely wounded in the leg. In November, 1903, he was made Lord Lieutenant of Nairn, as had so many of his predecessors. The "Pall Mall Gazette" noted ironically that it was unusual to have a Lord Lieutenant who was also a Subaltern, the relatively modest rank that Brodie then held in the Scots Guards.

Brodie Castle must have been a delightful place in Edwardian times. We hear of Butlers and French maids, the aroma of Russian cigarettes, of the gaiety of the flower shows in summer and the parties for local children at Christmas, with presents for everyone. Violet Hope was a familiar and popular figure, often to be seen driving her pony and trap in the lanes around Brodie. She had brought a stable lad with her from Rosehaugh who was to stay in service at the house for fifty years. Several fishing boats on the Moray Firth were named "Violet Hope" in her honour. Ian Brodie made a lasting reputation as a plant breeder, especially of daffodils. He produced over four hundred varieties in his lifetime, and planted them in great drifts around the Castle grounds.

The Edwardian Idyll ended, of course, in 1914. Elizabeth Baillie, the wife of the 22nd Laird passed over just before the outbreak of war with Germany. Her life had spanned the period from the Regency to the beginnings of motorised transport and manned flight...and the age of industrialised warfare. Ian Brodie of Brodie was mobilised in August 1914, as a Major in the Lovat Scouts. He served in the Dardanelles, Egypt and Palestine. He was mentioned in dispatches, awarded the Military Cross, and survived to return to Brodie. His Brother Douglas joined in 1915 and was killed on the Somme the following year. Another brother, Duncan, served in France, was twice wounded, mentioned in dispatches, and was also awarded the Military Cross. Their sister, Vere Brodie, joined up as a V.A.D. (Voluntary Aid Detachment) Nurse. She served in France and Belgium from 1915 until 1917, then as a. Unit

Administrator from 1918, including service with the allied army of occupation. Vere Brodie was chosen to represent her Service at the ceremony by which an Unknown British Soldier was chosen for interment in Westminster Abbey.

Ian and Violet had three sons, of whom the youngest, Ninian, became the 25th Brodie of Brodie. Ninian was educated at Eton and trained to the theatre, appearing at the Old Vic and in Repertory at Birmingham and Perth. He met his wife, Helena Budgen, when they played together in Rep at Perth. Ninian served in the Royal Artillery during the Second World War and became the Laird of Brodie when his father passed over in 1943. The Castle had been the Brodie's childhood home, so perhaps no one in the world knew or valued the old building so well. But the economic climate of post-war Britain was not promising for Brodie. Many great estates were ended during these years, by ruinous death duties and selective taxation. Even the relatively modern parts of Brodie Castle were in need of renovation.

The 22nd Laird's economies had not stood the test of time, and the Victorian parts of the house were now under attack by woodworm. The sandstone fabric of the building itself had become porous in places, and was deteriorating rapidly. The cost of repairs would be astronomical. The Government had provided a fund to purchase buildings of outstanding historical importance, and this, after years of negotiation, secured Brodie's future. The Castle and its contents were transferred to the National Trust for Scotland, and opened to the public.

The Brodie had secured his inheritance by parting with it; by doing so he ensured that the house would never be a ruin, and its contents and records would never be sold and dispersed. This security came at a high price, though. The castle was sold for a sum significantly lower than earlier valuations, and the contents - all the treasures of Brodie - had to be sold to the NTS to provide an endowment for future maintenance. So the heritage was secured for the nation, but the future Brodies of Brodie had lost their birthright.

This did not seem to trouble Alistair, the 26th Thane. He had little to do with the estate, but was a successful businessman and an early pioneer of computer technology. He survived his father by only seven months, and his son, Alexander, became the 27th Brodie of Brodie. He had fought a stubborn rearguard action through the Scottish courts to try to secure his inheritance, but without success.

8. BURGHEAD, JO'BURG, CHOLERA BAY

Just about the time that Elizabeth of Arnhall was getting married, and all unrecognised, events had begun locally that would change the course of Scotland's history. A few miles east of Brodie there was (and is) a farm called Inverugie. In the 1800's it was derelict, overblown with sand, and useless. This was a challenge to one of the leading improvers of the day, William Young. He knew that the soil beneath the sand was Moray's finest, and he was determined to bring it back into the light. So he employed men to dig trenches, sometimes eight feet deep, through the thin modem topsoil, through the layer of sterile sand, until they reached the ancient soil of the Laigh. They dug the good soil out, replaced the sand into the trench, and put the rich black earth back on top. It was a work of genius. Two hundred years later, Inverugie still thrives.

All along the coast, where the sea bites in to the sand, the hidden layer of good soil is exposed briefly to the light before being washed away. At Inverugie, Young demonstrated that men could reclaim what nature had buried. His improvements did not stop there. He took part in a syndicate of local businessmen (Which included his cousin, Patrick Sellar) that bought up the fishing village of Burghead, built a harbour, and swept away the ramshackle fishermen's huts. Burghead Well pre-dates the Roman occupation. It now sits among the neat stone cottages of Young's planned community. The fishermen there still carry out a pagan fire ritual at the New Year, called "Burning the Clavie" Now they carry the flaming tar barrel along Young Street and Sellar Street. Young had a second planned community constructed on his land, but no harbour was built there. Young over-extended himself financially, and went broke.

Although Young's improvements had not made him rich, they did bring him to the attention of Lord Stafford, who was married to the Countess of Sutherland. Stafford controlled the Sutherland estates, over seventeen hundred square miles of Northern Scotland. This vast inheritance brought in less than £1 per square mile in rents, and was obviously ripe for improvement. Stafford appointed Young and Sellar to make the land more productive, at least in money terms. Their idea of improvement was to evict the five thousand or so tenants, and let the vacant land as sheep farms to the highest bidder. They dealt with the practicalities of eviction personally, burning villages, employing troops and police as necessary, making thousands of Scots into refugees in their own land.

The Gordons of Cluny demonstrate the change in attitudes between the eighteenth and nineteenth centuries. The first Cluny, a close friend of the third Duke of Gordon, bought up land throughout the highlands when prices were low after the rebellion. His son, Cosmo Gordon, was a model landlord of the time. He allowed his tenants to pay their rent one year in arrears, which effectively capitalised their little farms and allowed them to prosper. But the third, Colonel John Gordon of Cluny, became known as the most vicious landlord in Victorian Britain. During the famine years of the 1840's he compelled starving families to "agree" to emigrate before he would allow them to receive aid. Those who tried to renege on the one-sided agreement were clubbed, bound, and forced aboard chartered emigrant ships with a savagery that beggars description. Many were penniless and dressed in rags. The ship's crew had to make clothes for them out of sail cloth and bread bags. Two thousand of Cluny's tenants were dumped on the coast of Canada, hungry, ragged, and penniless, with the Canadian winter before them. Many died. When the Colonel died, in 1858, he was the richest commoner in Scotland, with a fortune of over two million pounds sterling.

Mass Clearance does not seem to have occurred on the Laigh, which was always fortunate in its agriculture. The marginal upland areas took the brunt of the landlord's "Improvements." Even so, the local economy was severely affected by the influx of the destitute victims of clearance. A great bitterness grew among the people over the attitude of the established Church towards the evictions. Ministers were appointed by the patronage of the landowners, and rarely spoke against them. Some even preached sermons telling the displaced people to accept their fate as the Lord's will rather than the Laird's. This led to the great Schism in the Church remembered as "The Disruption," and the foundation of The Church of Scotland (Free). The Duchess of Gordon gave financial and moral support to the new Church and her Cousin the Brodie donated land for the construction of a free Church and manse to the east of Dyke village. The congregation remained split between the "East" and "West" churches until 1941, when the schism was finally reconciled. The newer "East" church is now an elegant holiday home, available for rent.

The late summer of 1829 brought another weather disaster of cataclysmic proportions to the people of the Laigh. Witnesses write of an immense black cloud, like a mountain, covering the South Western horizon. It brought the most violent storm in living memory. The wind rose to hurricane force, battering the merchant ships in the Firth and driving thirty of them to their destruction. A coal ship foundered with all hands within sight of Nairn Harbour, while the fishermen repeatedly tried to launch their boats in the crashing surf. Driving rain melted the snow on the peaks of Braemoray, causing the network of feeder streams to rise rapidly until they flowed "like mill spouts". The torrent cascaded down to the Laigh, swelling the rivers until they burst their banks.

Hundreds of trees were uprooted and swept along in the currents, smashing whatever they struck. Bridges and houses collapsed, embankments gave way, and the flood surged out over the surrounding fields. People, livestock, and wild animals alike struggled through the dark to find high ground. One man recalled afterwards how he and his wife were stranded on a hillock near the ruins of their home. *"Expecting every minute to be swept into eternity in such an unprepared state, and our lugs driven deaf wi' the roaring' o' the waters an' the crashing' o' the great trees that came bombing' past us ilka minute."* When asked if he had prayed he answered *"Aye Sir, Lang an' Strang."* When dawn came, it showed an inland sea, stretching from Kincorth to Forres. Twenty square miles of the Laigh were under water.

Many of the stranded families were rescued by fishing boats out of Findhorn, who sailed to their relief above the trees and fields of the parish. The log of the *"Nancy"* of Findhorn describes many such rescues;

"Tuesday, August 4th, 1829. Sailed from Findhorn at half past ten, a.m., wind blowing hard from N.N.E. In danger of foundering from trees and other land wreck running foul of us... tried to run up the channel of the Forres burn, but the strength of the current drove us on a bank, and nearly capsized us...set all sail, scudded, with a fair wind, over Mr.

Davidsons farm, and steered for a small house on the north side of Tannachty. Fell in with a very strong current there, but, by the efforts of all hands, fetched the house of Rory Fraser, shoemaker, his daughter and two children, who were sitting aloft on two or three deals (planks) with the water at their feet. Brought the stern of the boat to, and sang out to Rory. His daughter and her two laddies, making muckle din, were handed aboard. Rory himself was unco scared. The house had been shaking violently for the greater part of the night...made sail for the Turnpike, and as we got into the road, saw a man catch a fine salmon in one of the fields to starboard."

Seventy-five families in Dyke Parish were made destitute by the flood, and one hundred and eighty eight in the Parish of Forres. Yet the resilience of the people still shines through. Sir Thomas Dick Lauder published an account of the floods, which is packed with anecdotes of individual determination. An old man in a flooded cottage dives repeatedly beneath the turbid, flowing waters, until he recovers his spectacles. They were a gift from his son in Canada, and he would rather risk death than lose them. A young woman lifts her elderly parents to safety, showing almost superhuman strength, while she is immersed four foot deep in fast flowing water. A man wading chest deep, attempting to reach safety, still holds his umbrella open in a dogged attempt to keep his head dry. A man, who had been swept downstream in a rock filled torrent, and saved by a miracle, is asked what he thought of during his ordeal. *"Think of?"* He replies, *"Feggs, I was thinkin' how I could get out, and how I could catch my bonnet."*

The harvest was lost of course, both the standing crops and the stored. The landowners did what they could to help their tenants, but they had all suffered huge losses themselves, and many of the estates were already seriously burdened by debt. The Findhorn Bridge had been washed away, and was rebuilt by subscription by the local Gentry. We catch a glimpse of William, the 22nd Brodie, in the pages of the Inverness Courier, celebrating the opening of the new bridge in 1832. He leads the crowd of two thousand spectators in giving three hearty cheers; he dines, with his cousin Lethen, at the head of a table with 105 guests, and entertains the company afterwards by singing manly songs. All is gaiety and a proud sense of accomplishment. On the opposite page there is a two-line report of an outbreak of cholera at Fort William.

Cholera! Poverty was endemic in Scotland, made worse by the influx of poor wretches driven from the Glens. Their numbers swelled the populations of the towns, which were already overcrowded and unsanitary. There were no effective drainage systems in the poor areas, no piped water. Every cottage had a midden, or dunghill, outside, and the runoff was free to enter the watercourses. The outbreak reported so casually in the Courier was destined to kill 30,000 people. It struck hardest in the poor areas, and seems to have killed about one in three of those infected. Unfortunately, no one at the time understood the mechanism by which the disease was transmitted. It was widely believed to be an airborne contagion, and there remain eyewitness accounts of "Cholera Clouds" hanging over infected areas.

Great bonfires were piled up in the streets of Nairn and Forres and kept burning in an effort to drive the miasma away. We now know the disease to be carried by infected water supplies, which explains the concentration among the dwellings of the poor, with their ever-present middens. While local doctors laboured heroically to deal with the outbreak, the Inverness Courier printed some odd theories. One correspondent explained at length that the epidemic was God's way of leading the unrighteous to repentance, so that instead of deploring the outbreak as a calamity, we should hail it as a mercy. A short feature mentions that fifty refugees, fleeing from the "Infernal Places" of the Cholera, *"destitute of shelter, food or covering"* had been refused passage on the Meickle Ferry, and were obliged to go around by the hill country. There is no place of safety for them, no shelter or hospitality in their most Christian homeland.

There are numerous advertisements for emigrant ships in the same newspaper. They promise swift and comfortable passage to Canada, Australia, Tasmania or South Africa for those with the money to pay. There are glowing accounts of the comfortable lifestyle awaiting the emigrant overseas. The emigrant vessels on the Atlantic run were often timber ships that carried migrants on the outward voyage, and returned with lumber from the Canadian forests.

The passengers were stowed like cargo on wooden shelves in the timber holds. Rough weather could turn the ships into a floating hell, with the travelers shut below decks for days, and even weeks, at a time, without sanitation. The passengers suffered appallingly from the stench, the incessant violent motion, the sparse, mouldy food and tainted water. Many became so demoralised and exhausted that the first outbreak of fever quickly claimed them. It was reported in the House of Commons in 1848 that the death rate among those crossing the Atlantic was 17%.

During the famine years there were riots in Burghead as the people of the Laigh fought to prevent food being exported while they starved. The sailing vessel *Ceres*, moored in Young's harbour, was stormed by a mob that tried to unload her cargo of grain. The riot was put down by troops. A year later, the *Ceres* was an emigrant ship being used to ferry the "surplus population" across to Canada. There was no social provision for those left behind. The Courier records the death of Margaret Brodie of Drumeldrie, aged 70, in 1841. When, after a lifetime of hardship, she could no longer cope, she carefully laid out her best clothes, walked a little way from her house, and cut her own throat.

Moray Library Service has produced a collection of names and destinations of people from the North East who joined the exodus. There are pages of Gordons, Frasers, Campbells, a few Dunbars, Hays, Innes, Falconers, Forbes, all the names of the area. There are about forty Brodies. We may imagine some of them; a small, familiar looking group, plainly but respectably dressed, coming ashore at the Quarantine Station in Cholera Bay on Prince Edward Island, where the rough wooden crosses outside the fever hospital outnumber the living. They have turned their backs on their homeland, where poverty and injustice are their predetermined fate. They are facing a trek into the vast and ancient forests of the new world, where every ounce of their native thrift and hardiness will be needed just to survive, but which holds the promise of a free and independent future. With hard work, stoicism and luck they will create their own society. Generations of Brodies will be raised to live and die without ever seeing the Laigh of Moray. All will still share a name, a badge, a tartan, and a certain kinship.

A few Brodies had already made their mark in the New World. One

Colonel George Brodie of the Continental Army campaigned successfully against his former countrymen during the American War of Independence, and has a mountain in Massachusetts named after him. It is a popular Ski resort today, and it's owner, Matt Kelly, has given it a disconcerting Irish theme. Oh well. There were Brodies among those deported as slaves to the plantations after the Battle of Worcester, the '15 and the '45. George Brodie, a servant to Sir James Gordon of Park, was a prisoner of the 1715 rebellion, and John Brodie, a slater of Perth. There was an Alexander Brodie among the hapless Jacobites left behind in the garrison of Carlisle, and a John Brodie listed among the deportees to the Virginia plantations in 1747. The prisoners often married and settled among the other slaves, widening the ethnic base of the Scots abroad.

One of the leaders of the Jamaica slave revolt in 1830 was a Gordon, hanged by his white cousins from the yardarm of H.M.S. *Wolverine*. There were Brodies among the slave owners too, of Antigua and Jamaica. I wonder if they were ever disturbed by the familiar surnames among their "property". There were Brodies among the Canadian pioneers, including the epic settlement on the Red River. One of them, Neil Brodie, was captured by Poundmaker and spent twelve days as a prisoner of the Cree Nation. Back east at the same time was Steve Brodie, the New York Innkeeper who gave the American language the term *"Doing a Brodie"* by being the first man to jump off of the Brooklyn Bridge, 180 feet straight down into the East River. He then swam ashore to collect his bets. He subsequently demonstrated the protective qualities of a rubber suit, by claiming to have survived a trip over the Niagara Falls while wearing it, but no one believed him. I do. He was the original extreme sportsman, and may well have worn his Derby back to front and had "No Fear" embroidered on the back of his moleskin waistcoat.

Neil Brodie of Saskatchewan left a memoir of his experiences during the North West Rebellion in Canada during the 1880's. Neil made his living as a freighter, driving the great ox-wagons over the harsh rock-and-water terrain between Regina (then called *Pile o' Bones*) and Calgary. The steady westward advance of the settlers had been greatly assisted by the opening of the Canadian Pacific Railroad, itself the brainchild of a Forres man, Donald Smith, who was born in a little cottage by the Muckle Burn and lived to become Lord Strathcona, one of the founders of modern Canada. The spread of the settlers put pressure on the local peoples, the Cree Indians and the mixed-race Metis, who lived by hunting and needed a lot of space. They had rebelled once before, and extracted concessions from the British Empire. At that time there were very few settlers in those parts, centred around the Red River, and British political opinion had tended to favour native rights. The rebel leader, Louis Riel, became a folk hero of the Metis, and they brought him out of retirement to lead the second rebellion in 1885. Riel had gone a bit batty during his years in exile, and returned to Canada believing himself to be the new Messiah. He had two main concentrations of earthly force, his own Metis and the Cree Indians under their Chief, Poundmaker.The rebels spent a few weeks massacring settlers and capturing the thinly defended outposts of the Saskatchewan Valley; and Riel thought that he had outmanoeuvred Queen Victoria once again. He declared the North West Territory to be an independent state with himself as it's religious and political leader. Ironically, the railway that had started the whole sorry business now carried troops, and they would end his peoples way of life. In May, 1885, three government columns entered the valley, firing as they came. Neil Brodie was freighting supplies intended for one of the columns, driving a team in a convoy of twenty wagons. On the morning of the 14th May he was among the tree-crowned bluffs of the Eagle Hills about twelve miles south of Battleford, when the convoy was ambushed. The drivers ran their oxen into a circle with the wagons outside, and fought a desperate defensive action, with just ten rifles, against more than three hundred Cree warriors. It could not last long. When the Indians offered parley, the drivers accepted, and Neil Brodie became a prisoner of the Cree nation. He was taken to their camp, running at the stirrup of his captor's horse. The Indians held a Council at the Camp, to decide what to do with the prisoners. They sat, morbidly fascinated, watching a debate in a language they did not understand, but upon which their very lives depended. Brodie later wrote:

"If a speaker wanted to kill us, he would dance around with his rifle in the hollow of his arm and speak loud and fast. If he was willing to spare our lives, he would leave his rifle on the ground and walk around the

circle and talk quietly. Finally they agreed to keep us alive if none of us tried to run away. If any did, then the blood-thirsty had the privilege of killing the rest. We, of course, accepted these terms. "

Brodie was robbed of everything he possessed. It took a lot of beating and threats to make him give up his thirty-four dollars in cash, which he wryly attributed to his Scots upbringing. One of his fellow captives had his watch, a family heirloom, stolen, and two hours later saw the cogs and springs of it being used to ornament a warrior's hair. The Cree women were kind to Neil Brodie, giving him food. One old woman caught him by the wrist and rubbed his hand over her head in a mute display of empathy. The men were generally less sympathetic, although Brodie remembered one Indian called Jacob that brought the prisoners some clothes to replace those that his fellows had plundered. Another of the warriors saw Brodie shivering with the cold and brought him a rabbit skin blanket *"..under which I went sound asleep and forgot all my troubles."* Brodie described a few of his captors in his memoir. He described Poundmaker as:

"...a very fine looking Indian. Tall, with very long hair hanging in two braids in front. Dressed in blanket chaps, moccasins, cow hide waistcoat covered with rows of round headed brass tacks; sometimes carrying his Pukamakin "

Brodie described another warrior as *"...a real dandy who could speak many languages...he told me he had killed one poor devil...they called this Indian General Gordon"* ... a new variation on an ancient theme. The following day, Brodie heard shots, and was told that a trooper of the Royal Canadian Mounted Police had been killed. The Cree warriors had stalked the redcoat through the woods and shot him through the back of the head. He never knew that they were there. They buried him under a mound of earth carried from a badger set. Soon after runners arrived with news that Riel had been defeated, and was a prisoner of the British. The Indians held another council, and decided to take the prisoners to Battleford to ask for terms. Brodie's ordeal had lasted just twelve days.

Well, Brodie survived the experience and lived to see Riel hang. He saw General Gordon hang, too, wearing a new pair of moccasins that his sweetheart had made him for his last journey. He was present at the trial of the Indian Chiefs, and noted that the charge of "High Treason" was translated into the Cree language as *"Throwing sticks at Queen Victoria and trying to knock her bonnet off."* Neil Brodie survived the frontier days and lived on into the modern age, writing his memoirs of the rebellion in 1932. He retained his native love of genealogy, enquiring into the forbears of the editor of the Saskatchewan Herald while arranging to have his memoir printed. By then the Scots had made great improvements to the social and agricultural economy of Canada...at the price of driving off the native peoples and destroying their way of life, making them into refugees in their own country. There were no emigrant ships or new worlds for the native peoples.

Doctor William Hampden Brodie was the great, great Grandson of William Brodie of Glenbuchat, who had stood in the rebel lines at Culloden. He was thereby a descendant of the 12th laird, Alexander of the Bloodfeud days. William studied medicine at Aberdeen University, graduating as a Doctor in 1882. After visiting America, he made his way to the South African Goldfields, settling in the frontier boom-town of Johannesburg. He became the Medical Officer of the Ferreira group of mines. The Transvaal at that time was not a part of the British Empire, although there was a hazy reference in its constitution to the suzerainety of Queen Victoria. The Province was ruled with a grim, old-testament integrity by the Boers under their president Paul Kruger, who had led the guerrilla war that had repelled earlier attempts at incursion by the British. The Boers were a high-minded people in matters of money, but they could scarcely ignore the fact that their farms were positioned above the richest gold deposits on Earth. They allowed British Capital to finance the mining operations, and British engineers to develop the mines, but they categorised the incomers as "Uitlanders", the political and social inferiors to the chosen Boers, and they denied them political representation. The subjects of the Queen - Empress were not minded to accept such treatment from the farmers, and the British people considered the Boer ownership of the gold deposits to be a historical mistake in need of correction. The Johannesburg Reform Committee was formed, to agitate for political change, and William Brodie became a leading member. The Committee was mostly made up of professional men from the smart Jo'burg suburb of Doorfontein, but it included Frank Rhodes, the younger Brother of the great Empire Builder Cecil Rhodes (then the richest man in the world) and two brothers, the elder being Doctor Leander Starr Jameson, who was to lead the farcical tragedy remembered as Jameson's Raid. Jameson was physically small and rather wistful looking, but he was a lifelong gambler with a persuasive tongue. He argued for a bold, piratical stroke to secure the gold fields for Britain. The Uitlanders were to rise in arms against the Boers, and when Kruger retaliated a force led by Jameson would invade the Transvaal and come to their relief, dragging the British Government into a war that it must ultimately win. The Committee agreed the plan, and Jameson returned to British South Africa to raise his invasion force.

Jameson was too much of a dreamer. He used his contacts with Rhodes to raise about five hundred good men of the British South Africa Company Police, but officered them with a rag-bag of young fellows looking for adventure. They had a twelve pounder field gun and five Maxim machine guns, which seemed to Jameson to be adequate to deal with the Boers. But the Committee in Jo'burg knew better. As Jameson rode with his force to the Transvaal border, Brodie and his colleagues cabled him urgently to postpone the raid, to give them more time to prepare, but they were too late. The rising went off at half cock, and failed. The Reform Committee had to negotiate an armistice or face extinction. The raiders crossed the border without opposition, but as they penetrated deeper into the Veldt on tired horses, they found themselves flanked by Boer veterans, who poured fire into their ranks and then melted back into the bush. The raid ended in ignominious failure, and the British Government abandoned the conspirators to their fate. Brodie was sent to prison. The "Transvaal Leader" newspaper said of him:

"No man in Johannesburg could have been freer from bitter feelings against his fellow colonists belonging to the older population. At the same time he felt, like his co-reformers, that the Johannesburg people would not continue to accept the status of outlanders without sacrifice of their self-respect. Nobody had a stouter heart for the risks of revolution, and when these risks matured he made light of his imprisonment as a holiday he had been needing for a good many years. "

The Brodies always seem to get a good write-up, when they go to jail. Of course, Jameson's Raid was disowned by Government, but not by the people of Britain, who saw it as a failed but worthy attempt to assert Britain's right to keep Africa British. The Poet Laureate summed up the popular feeling:

Let Lawyers and Statesmen addle their pates over points of law;

If sound be our sword and saddle and gun-gear, who cares one straw?

When men of our own blood pray us to ride to their kinfolks aid

Not heaven itself shall stay us From the rescue they call a raid.

A sentiment worthy of the 12th Thane himself, and equally anachronistic. It led, in time, to the Boer war, in every sense the Vietnam of the British Empire. William spent that campaign aboard the hospital ship *"Lismore Castle"*, treating the grievous wounds of war in the tropical heat, without antibiotics, and in later years he regretted the raid and all that had come of it. He came to know Paul Kruger, the dour, hard-bitten prophet of the Afrikaner State, and, over a cup of coffee, Kruger told him that he had always admired the Scots, and suspected that he was himself descended from their stock. William died of pneumonia in 1909. The Transvaal Leader wrote generously of his sane outlook, cheerful humour and kindly temperament.

Doctor Benjamin Collins Brodie sprang from a southern branch, his family having moved to England from Banff during the 1740's. Benjamin's father was the Rector of Winterslow in Wiltshire. Benjamin had an excellent start, educated at Charterhouse and Oxford, and became the most distinguished surgeon of the Victorian age. He operated to remove a tumour from the scalp of George IV, and became a favourite with the King, ultimately attending him throughout his final illness. When William IV became King, Brodie was appointed Royal Surgeon (another Brodie was the Royal Chaplain), and two years later he was made a Baronet. Brodie was a cool and determined hand as a surgeon, but his chief skill lay in diagnosis and in research. He published several on physiology and comparative anatomy that have stood the test of time, and his research into disease prevention laid the foundations of a new discipline. His son, Sir Benjamin Collins Brodie the younger, also became a distinguished research scientist, particularly remembered for his work in resolving the chemical properties of hydrocarbons.

Alexander and William Brodie, two sons of a Banff Shipmaster, both became successful sculptors. The Statue of the Duke of Richmond that gazes benevolently across the square in Huntly is Alexander's work, as is the marble statue of Queen Victoria in Aberdeen. He did a lot of small, sentimental pieces like the "Highland Mary" and "Motherless Lassie" that remain as priceless evocations of Victorian taste. His brother William specialised in portrait busts, and his bust of Queen Victoria is still displayed at Balmoral. He is responsible for the enormous statue of Prince Albert at Perth, and several smaller statues around Edinburgh. Both the brothers began their careers as trade apprentices, and they rose to distinction through talent and hard work.

There are about six thousand Brodie households in the world today. Most could trace their origins back to the Laigh of Moray, perhaps to the banks of the Muckle Burn. To those who have with Wallace bled, those whom Bruce has often led. The Brodies of Brodie were party to many of the great events of Scots and British history, well known to Mary Stuart and James VI, a ray of hope for Charles I and a pain to Charles II, loyal allies to the house of Hanover in the Jacobite years, staunch Tories of the Landed Gentry in Victorian times. Their children and their Clansmen helped to build the British Empire, and now raise their families in every part of the English speaking world. Six thousand separate sagas, linked by a common thread.

My own great-grandfather, William Brodie, was a ploughman at a farm by Port Tannachy, in the Enzie, East of the Spey. He was lucky to have well paid and respectable employment in the countryside during the 1880's, although the dear knows that he had little leisure time:

Six days shalt thou labour and do all that thou are able,

On the seventh day wash the horses legs, and tidy up the stable

His son, my Grandfather, Alexander William Brodie, had the tenancy of a 70 acre farm called Mosshead, just outside Huntly. The old house is still there, used as a store by the much larger farm that has swallowed up Mosshead and its former neighbours. That house was the childhood home of my father, Alexander William Brodie. He used to visit family (Gordons) around Burghead, and explored the Laigh of Moray on his push bike during the golden summers between the wars. I have a picture of him, aged about fourteen, barefoot in a field with a push-hoe in his hands. It is early Spring, and it must have been freezing outdoors, and the soil beneath his feet is riddled with large stones, but he smiles at his dad with the camera. He joined the Gordon Highlanders as a regular in 1937, and served with them in the B.E.F., North Africa and Sicily before taking part in the D-Day landings. He was seriously wounded in the fight for Caen, and was believed killed for three months, until he woke up in a Canadian Hospital and was able to tell them who he was. He finished the war as a Sergeant instructor, and had a peacetime career as a transport manager in a firm of hauliers.

I visited Brodie for the first time in 1986, with a vague idea of showing my two sons, born and raised in England, something of the Scottish side of their heritage. They were young enough to display an uncomplicated delight in seeing their name on road signs and destination boards, and especially, on a castle with battlements, towers and turrets. As we stood among a group of visitors looking at the Van Dyke portrait of Charles I, the guide asked me, (out of the blue and in front of about twenty people) if I was a Brodie. *I am,* says I, *and why do you ask?* - she replies, *I thought so, you look like a Brodie.* General merriment and some embarrassment, and a new agenda when looking at the portraits. (It's the nose, by the way, Archibald Campbell's nose.) After at least five generations of absence, my branch of the Clan are still recognised locally. And indeed, I once met a James Robert Brodie in Lancaster, no traceable relation, who looked like my brother. So one pool of the Muckle Burn, the Gene pool, is still producing the recognisable article wherever it has flowed. Long may it continue to do so. I can hear my father and his toast at the family Christmas dinner:

"Here's tae us!... Whae's like us?

Gey Few!"

9. BRODIE COUNTRY

The view across the Laigh of Moray from the road outside Nairn is one of the most beautiful in Scotland, and it is worth seeing for yourself

There is a small local museum in Nairn that is well worth a visit. Part of the Duchess of Gordon's mineral collection is on display there, as are a few relics recovered from the Culbin Sands, including the plough that was abandoned in the sandstorm. The Museum has an excellent collection of books on local history, which includes some very rare items indeed, which visitors are allowed to consult. But if you don't want to spend your hols in museums and libraries, Nairn is a nice town with good beaches and makes an excellent touring base. The field of Culloden, of course, is just outside the town, as are the bronze age tombs of the Clava Cairns. Nearby, Kilravock is open as a hotel, set in beautiful grounds. The woods are a carpet of bluebells in the Spring.

Of course, you'll want to visit the highlands. Well, Inverness is the capital of the highlands, and it is only ten miles or so from Nairn, perhaps fifteen from Brodie. If you take the road through the Great Glen, it's only about twenty miles to Glenmoriston. You can be as academic or as trivial as you like there, since it is at the very hub of the highlands. The Loch Ness Visitor Centre and the picturesque ruin of Urquhart Castle are both nearby, with excellent food and drink at the Glenmoriston Hotel. The scenery of the Loch is always stunning, and it is at it's most impressive when the weather is overcast.

I dived Loch Ness in '88, to find a cave where a Victorian Diver, working on the wreck of a paddle steamer, claimed to have seen the monster. The steamer wreck is still on the Admiralty chart, although only a few plates and ribs remain on the 7 metre shelf where she sank. The bulk of her remains have gone over the edge of the shelf, a sheer drop of a thousand feet down to the floor of the Loch. The water is peat-stained to the colour of strong black tea, so it is necessary to use a torch even in shallow water in daytime. It was easy to find the cave, in the steep rock wall just inshore of the wreck site. It was precisely as described in the Victorian account, including the narrow ledge where a creature with a head like a huge frog had leered at the diver and sent him back to the surface like a prototype Polaris. The shelf was empty now, but the confirmation of the circumstantial details of the sighting so long before made the dive feel distinctly eerie. So did a very short exploration of the precipice. We swam out over the edge and dropped down to fifteen metres. At that depth it was midnight black, and the rock face picked out in our torch beams was also black, glass smooth and near-vertical. The sense of the Abyss forbade further exploration - we had to get back to the daylight. Mind you, not all Scottish diving is quite so atmospheric. The Sea diving around Oban and the inner Hebrides is superb, and there are day trips to the islands, including Iona, every day from Oban Harbour.

Above the surface, there is some magnificent scenery on the little-used road that runs up the eastern side of the Loch. This was Simon Fraser's country in the Jacobite years, and the landscape would be completely familiar to him; but how shocked he would be to find it virtually uninhabited!. He was so keen to expand the numbers of his Clan that he would wine and dine any tenant that would change his family name to Fraser. Now the hills are empty and the few cottages still visible are slowly sinking back into the earth. You can often see the pattern of the runrig fields in the grass on the hillsides, but the only tenants are the sheep. There were a lot of Frasers among the highlanders that stormed the Heights of Abraham with Wolfe, and subsequently opened up the Canadian west. The Fraser River is named for a Strathglass Tacksman that found himself running the rapids to the Pacific in a birch bark canoe. How often the Scots abroad must have dreamed of these hills, that would have seemed to them as familiar and comforting as a mothers face.

I doubt if many people dreamed longingly of Lochindorb, the Lake of Troubles where the Wolf of Badenoch had his lair. The high moor where the lake is situated could be used as the set for a Dracula film. The clear loch echoes the enormous bowl of sky, mirrors the low grey racing clouds that promise a chilling downpour. Up here it is always colder and windier than down on the Laigh, and many of the surrounding slopes are little but lifeless scree. A local farmer has a boat you can hire at a modest price to fish the cold, crystal clear loch, and you can land on the island to examine the Castle. There is a scrubby sort of wild red cabbage that grows among the ruins, known as Lochindorb Kail, it is not particularly prepossessing, but the island is the only place on earth where it grows, and it may be a mediaeval ancestor of some of our more familiar cabbages. Perhaps the Wolf of Badenoch enjoyed a helping of it with his roast beef or boar, or baby. I would not call Lochindorb beautiftil, but it has atmosphere, an authentic evocative mediaeval landscape.

The road to Forres takes you from Lochindorb down the valley of the Dorback, and so to the Findhom. Once off the moor the route is well wooded to the point of being a deciduous jungle. The road passes Altyre, where the twelfth and thirteenth Thanes of Brodie went roaring into battle with the Cummings, and a small diversion takes us to the watch tower above the church at Ardclach, a most romantic spot. The road climbs steeply and curves tightly, as if the hill were conical, but little can be seen through the dense woodland that grows right up to the tarmac of the single track road and joins its boughs overhead. A deer and a pheasant at the roadside look up as the car passes, but do not run. A hare runs jinking along the road right in the cars path, and I brake until he finally darts into the wood. A track to the left is marked by a post from which a huge iron key hangs in a glass fronted box. A hand written note politely asks visitors to remember to lock the tower up again, and return the key. Such evidence of trust adds to the sense of a special, perhaps unique place.

Leaving the car and clambering up the steep path, the trees thin out and there is the tower. Two stories of whitewashed stone, a steep roof with a crow-stepped gable, a belfiy at one end and stone steps up to the entrance. There is a pleasant raised and levelled area at the front of the tower which says "Patio" to the modern mind, until the modern mind starts working again and answers "Gun emplacement". It all faces across the valley to the steep hill on the other side, perhaps a mile horizontally but three, four times that, if you had to scramble down through the wood and up the other side. That slope opposite was Levrattich *"The Heathy slope of the flag"* where forward lookouts could be posted in times of tension and give the alarm by waving a flag on the slope below the level of the skyline, visible to the watchers in the tower but not to the approaching caterans. And what then? A quiet alarm, preparation, ambush?. Grim work in this idyllic setting, for sure. The big iron key turns smoothly in the lock. In front there is a staircase, to the right a pitch dark room with a flagged floor. This was used as a lock up, a convenient holding cell. Up the stairs there is a more congenial room, with a large fire place and a certain amount of light and ventilation provided by gun loops and tiny barred lookout windows. Over the fireplace the entwined monogram of Alexander and Margaret Brodie of Lethen, who rebuilt this tower after it had been destroyed by caterans. This tower was built to be defended, and to endure. It is three and a half centuries old, built before the great fire of London, and it is as strong and comfortable (upstairs) as the day it was completed..

The road back to Forres passes close to Dulsie Bridge, which has a fine view of the confluence of the Divie and the Dorback. The peat stained waters burst white as they meet the rocks in the river bed, and set up a fascinating pattern of whirlpools and eddies. It can be very dramatic in the Spring and autumn spates. The slope at the lower end of the bridge was known as a fairy hill in more superstitious times. Scots fairies, naturally, were not the simpering milk-and water creatures of the southern imagination. They were more in the way of goblins, vicious and spiteful. The viewpoint over the gorge is on land belonging to today's Brodies of Lethen. Robert Burns dallied here, and made written notes on the sights and sounds of the Findhorn Gorge, although they never became verse. The route passes close to Randolph's Leap, hidden from the road in the deep canopy of trees. Doctor Johnson remarked on the lack of mature trees in the Scotland of his day, so he would scarcely recognise this part of his journey. There were twelve million trees planted on the Damaway Estate alone in the nineteenth century, and the rising ground between the Laigh and Braemoray is one huge deciduous forest, quite apart from the nine square miles of Culbin. The sound of the wind in their boughs is like the earth breathing.

The village of Dyke has about six hundred inhabitants today, less than a third of the eighteenth century population. It is a neat, quiet, well-kept and prosperous place. The Parish Church stands on a gentle rise in the middle of the village. It is a large, plain building, with a belfry at one end. An ornate family vault outside the Church houses the Earls of Moray. It was originally inside the earlier, heather-roofed Kirk that the "Bonnie Earl's" contemporaries and killers would have known. Strange to think of them walking up this same path across the Kirkyard. The path where Alexander, the 15th Thane, turned back to defy the tyranny of Charles II. Where Mary Sleigh grieved for her headstrong husband and her doomed children, and where so many have come to pray for peace down the war-ravaged centuries.

The bulk of the present church dates from 1781, although parts of the earlier building were incorporated in the new. There has been a church on the site since the very beginning of Christianity in Scotland, and Dyke is particularly associated with Saint Moluag, a travelling missionary of the seventh Century. Saint Columba is said to have made more than one visit here, and to have used the Findhorn valley as his route down to the Laigh. The Church has been constantly re-inventing itself since, and continues to do so. Inside all is bright and cheerful, with children's drawings on the wall and a bright orange carpet in the vestry. A gaily coloured curtain covers a tombstone set into the wall. It marks the long home of Ricardus Brothy, Richard Brodie, and his unnamed wife, who were married in 1446. The Christian Cross that is carved the full height and width of the stone is narrow as a sword, with curved finials at the end of each arm. Our guide tells us that this type of cross traditionally marks the grave of a Crusader. Was this a symbolic tribute, or did Richard wield his sword beneath the blazing skies of the holy land?. Five Centuries have obscured the inscription, and part of it is completely unreadable. Another memorial announces that Kinnaird of Culbin and his wife, Elizabeth Innes "Made this bed of stone" in 1613. Now their mansion sleeps, too, deep in the sand beneath the Culbin Forest.

In the main body of the church, the seats are arranged along the longest axis, and facing the pulpit, with curved rows of seats on the ground floor and raised galleries above, with access stairs at either end. The pulpit is an ancient three-decker affair, the top position being for the Minister, and the intermediate for the precentor, who would lead the congregation in the singing of psalms without musical accompaniment. The bottom position is the stool of penitence, where the hapless sinners of the parish would have to sit wearing sackcloth in the face of the congregation for a prescribed number of Sundays. Only two examples of this type of pulpit have survived in Scotland. This one may date back to the 15th Laird's time, and it is still in weekly use. I ask to see the entrance to the family vault of the Brodies of Brodie. I expect to see a noble stone sepulchre. The carpet in the vestry is pulled back, and a hatch in the floor raised, to show a flight of worn stone steps leading down into darkness. It is unadorned, matter of fact, Presbyterian. We replace the trapdoor quietly, and push the carpet back.

The Castle Railway Station is now called "Invercairn House" a comfortable and modestly priced bed and breakfast hotel, virtually at the gates of the Castle. Over the road is the Old Mill Inn, a large and friendly hostelry with a good range of draught ales. It has a pleasant garden for the long summer evenings. Brodie itself is a prosperous little place, with one really outstanding shop, specialising in country produce. They sell everything from a single Malt (Brodie Whisky!) to fresh vegetables, to framed water colours of the surrounding area. They have a nice book shop too, and a rather classy gift section. It is all within a few minutes' walk of the Castle grounds. Just inside the gate of the castle is the Rodney Stone, the enigmatic Pictish cross slab. The drive then continues through dense evergreen woodland until the trees start to thin out where the visitor car parks have been provided. There is a children's play area and a few pleasant picnic tables set around the edges of the wood. The house looks magnificent, the pale pink of its rendered surfaces contrasting with the well kept lawns to its front. Inside, a small army of neat, efficient guides are at hand to show the visitor around. The building is preserved as a late Victorian mansion rather than its earlier forms - there are tower houses nearby at Burgie and Coxton, that will give an impression of the Brodie of the Bloodfeud days. Now the tower is incorporated with the later additions in a seamless blend. Do not miss the small water-colour in the guard chamber, showing the "Brodie Castle" built in Madras two hundred years ago. The chamber still has the original gun- loops for windows. The rooms themselves are beautifully presented, as individual and precious as jewels. The dining room is laid out as for a grand dinner party, the table radiant with silver, porcelain and crystal. The blue sitting room is as precious as a Faberge egg, with the 15th Thane's ornamental ceiling, a rich blue nineteenth century wallpaper, and a delicate assembly of fine antique furniture and porcelain. The Red Drawing room, once the Laird's chamber, is virtually a picture gallery, and includes a small portrait of Montrose. The Victorian drawing room contains the carpet bought at the Great Exhibition, and a selection of exquisite furniture and fittings, including a noble carved fireplace. The Opie portrait of the Madras children is displayed here, and a Romney portrait of "Bonnie Jane", the fourth Duchess of Gordon. Small portraits allow us to glimpse the features of George Gordon, Anne Storey, Elizabeth Baillie, so many of the actors on this historic stage. The 15th Thane's portrait of Charles I is also displayed here. In the library, note the letter from the Bruce displayed under glass, and the chair from Deacon Brodie's shop in Edinburgh. It often used to be Ninian, the 25th Brodie, who took the money at the door, or identified the people in the portraits to the visitors. He was quite a raconteur, too, often telling interesting stories and sometimes risque anecdotes... the 25th Brodie decided to share the magnificence of his home with the rest of the world, and by doing so saved it for the future. He has earned the gratitude of all who have, by the virtue of their name, a small stake in the history of the Clan and Family of Brodie.

Printed in Great Britain
by Amazon